Solomon

The queen of Sheba pays homage to Solomon, as described in 1 Kings10:2, in this painting from the 15th century.

Money at its Best:
Millionaires of the Bible

Abraham and Sarah   Joseph

Daniel   Moses

David   Noah

Esther   Samson

Jacob   Solomon

Job   Wealth in Biblical Times

MONEY
at its
BEST

Solomon

Jennifer Vance

Mason Crest Publishers
Philadelphia

Produced by OTTN Publishing.
Cover design © 2008 TLC Graphics, www.TLCGraphics.com.

Mason Crest Publishers
370 Reed Road, Suite 302
Broomall PA 19008
www.masoncrest.com

First printing

1 3 5 7 9 8 6 4 2

Library of Congress Cataloging-in-Publication Data

  Vance, Jennifer.
    Solomon / Jennifer Vance.
       p. cm. — (Millionaires of the Bible: money at its best)
    Includes bibliographical references and index.
    ISBN 978-1-4222-0476-4 (alk. paper)
    ISBN 978-1-4222-0851-9 (pbk. : alk. paper)
    1. Solomon, King of Israel. I. Title.
    BS580.S6V36 2008
    222'.53092—dc22
                                        2008011687

Table of Contents

Solomon and His Wealth

- When Solomon became king of Israel, he inherited not only the throne, but also the vast wealth of his father, David. King David attributed his wealth and position to his close relationship to God, and advised his son to obey God so as not to lose God's blessings: "Walk in his ways, and keep his decrees and commands, his laws and requirements, as written in the Law of Moses, so that you may prosper in all you do and wherever you go." (1 Kings 2:2)

- In the beginning of Solomon's reign, God appeared to Solomon, and offered him his heart's desire. Solomon asked for the gift of wisdom. God was pleased. "Since you have asked for this and not for long life or wealth for yourself . . . I will give you a wise and discerning heart, so that there will never have been anyone like you, nor will there ever be. Moreover, I will give you what you have not asked for—both riches and honor—so that in your lifetime you will have no equal among kings." (1 Kings 3:11-13)

- Solomon increased his wealth by marrying the Egyptian pharaoh's daughter. Her father gave Solomon a whole city as a wedding present (the captured Canaanite city of Gezer). Solomon also received yearly tribute from the Philistines and other countries that were under his rule.

- Solomon's home would have been a showplace for his immense wealth. The Bible says Solomon's palace was built with stone and cedar wood, and decorated with gold and precious stones. In addition, Solomon built the Jewish Temple, and filled it with ornate bronze sculptures, statues, and pillars made by skilled craftsmen. The Temple also featured furnishings made of pure gold, and a room covered in gold, described in I Kings 6-7.

- Solomon often received gifts from other rulers, such as the fabled Queen of Sheba, who gave the king more than four tons of gold, large quantities of spices, and precious stones.

- Solomon remained wealthy for the rest of his life; however, he displeased God in his later years by worshipping other gods. "So the Lord said to Solomon, "Since this is your attitude and you have not kept my covenant and my decrees, which I commanded you, I will most certainly tear the kingdom away from you and give it to one of your subordinates." (1 Kings 11:11) Solomon's descendants would suffer the consequences of his actions, and would eventually lose their inheritance—their kingdom—and the wealth of Solomon.

Introduction: Wealth and Faith

Many people believe strongly that great personal wealth is incompatible with deep religious belief—that like oil and water, the two cannot be mixed. Christians, in particular, often feel this way, recollecting Jesus Christ's own teachings on wealth. "Do not store up for yourselves treasures on earth, where moth and rust destroy, and where thieves break in and steal," Jesus cautions during the Sermon on the Mount (Matthew 6:19). In Luke 18:25, he declares, "It is easier for a camel to go through the eye of a needle than for a rich man to enter the kingdom of God"—a sentiment repeated elsewhere in the Gospels.

Yet in Judeo-Christian culture there is a long-standing tradition of material wealth as the manifestation of God's blessing. This tradition is amply reflected in the books of the Hebrew Bible (or as Christians know them, the Old Testament). Genesis 13:2 says that the patriarch Abram (Abraham) "had become very wealthy in livestock and in silver and gold"; the Bible makes it clear that this prosperity is a gift from God. Other figures whose lives are chronicled in

Genesis—including Isaac, Jacob, Joseph, Noah, and Job—are described as both wealthy and righteous. The book of Deuteronomy expresses God's promise of prosperity for those who obey his commandments:

> If you fully obey the Lord your God and carefully follow all his commands I give you today, the Lord your God will set you high above all the nations on earth. . . . The Lord will grant you abundant prosperity—in the fruit of your womb, the young of your livestock and the crops of your ground—in the land he swore to your forefathers to give you. (Deuteronomy 28:1, 11)

A key requirement for this prosperity, however, is that God's blessings must be used to help others. Deuteronomy 15:10–11 says, "Give generously . . . and do so without a grudging heart; then because of this the Lord your God will bless you in all your work and in everything you put your hand to." The book of Proverbs—written during the time of Solomon, one of history's wealthiest rulers—similarly presents wealth as a desirable blessing that can be obtained through hard work, wisdom, and following God's laws. Proverbs 14:31 promises, "The faithless will be fully repaid for their ways, and the good man rewarded for his."

Numerous stories and folktales show the generosity of the patriarchs. According to Jewish legend, Job owned an inn at a crossroads, where he allowed travelers to eat and drink at no cost. When they offered to pay, he instead told them about God, explaining that he was simply a steward of the wealth that God had given to him and urging them to worship God, obey God's commands, and receive their own blessings. A story about Abraham says that when he moved his flocks from one field to another, he would muzzle the animals so that they would not graze on a neighbor's property.

After the death of Solomon, however, the kingdom of Israel

was divided and the people fell away from the commandments God had mandated. The later writings of the prophets, who are attempting to correct misbehavior, specifically address unethical acts committed to gain wealth. "You trample on the poor," complained the prophet Amos. "You oppress the righteous and take bribes and you deprive the poor of justice in the courts" (Amos 5:11, 12). The prophet Isaiah insists, "Learn to do right! Seek justice, encourage the oppressed. . . . If you are willing and obedient, you will eat the best from the land; but if you resist and rebel, you will be devoured by the sword" (Isaiah 1:17, 19–20).

Viewed in this light, the teachings of Jesus take on new meaning. Jesus does not condemn wealth; he condemns those who would allow the pursuit of wealth to come ahead of the proper relationship with God: "No one can serve two masters. . . . You cannot serve both God and money" (Matthew 6:24).

Today, nearly everyone living in the Western world could be considered materially wealthier than the people of the Bible, who had no running water or electricity, lived in tents, walked when traveling long distances, and wore clothing handmade from animal skins. But we also live in an age when tabloid newspapers and trashy television programs avidly follow the misadventures of spoiled and selfish millionaire athletes and entertainers. In the mainstream news outlets, it is common to read or hear reports of corporate greed and malfeasance, or of corrupt politicians enriching themselves at the expense of their constituents. Often, the responsibility of the wealthy to those members of the community who are not as successful seems to have been forgotten.

The purpose of the series MONEY AT ITS BEST: MILLIONAIRES OF THE BIBLE is to examine the lives of key figures from biblical history, showing how these people used their wealth or their powerful and privileged positions in order to make a difference in the lives of others.

This marble sculpture represents Solomon, who ruled the kingdom of Israel more than 2,900 years ago. Solomon is often considered to be the wisest and wealthiest ruler in history.

SOLOMON THROUGH THE AGES

Solomon appears in stories from three of the world's major religions: Judaism, Christianity, and Islam. He is portrayed as a wealthy, powerful, and diplomatic leader; a prolific writer; and a forerunner in municipal building projects. While Solomon is most certainly known for these qualities, he is best known for his extreme powers of deduction and his far-reaching wisdom. Purportedly, Solomon was the wisest person who has ever lived. Though Solomon's kingdom has faded and many of the things he actually wrote have been lost to the passage of time, stories about his knowledge, wealth, and power have survived nearly 3,000 years after his death.

The Bible says that Solomon's wisdom was a gift granted by God after he ascended the throne of his father David to become the king of Israel. However, other legends depict Solomon's wisdom as an innate ability only strengthened by God's gift. Of the biblical stories concerning Solomon's wisdom, one is most often remembered. It is the story presented in 1 Kings 3 concerning a dispute between two women.

According to the story in the Bible, each woman had an infant child. After one of the children died in the middle of the night, both women claimed to be the surviving child's mother. Since the women could not reach an agreement, they appeared in court before Solomon, asking him to resolve their dispute. When Solomon asked for a sword to cut the child in half so both women could have half of the living child, the child's real mother begged him not to hurt the child. She was even willing to let the other woman have him to keep the child safe. Thus, by using deductive reasoning and his knowledge of a mother's love for her child, Solomon was able to restore the child to his rightful mother.

Similar stories exist in folktales such as those contained in Hayyim Nahman Bialik's *And It Came to Pass: Legends and Stories About King David and King Solomon*. One such story, "The Inheritance," concerns a merchant whose son was away on a voyage when he died. The father entrusted his estate to his favorite servant with instructions that everything should be given to the son upon his return. However, since the servant was dishonest at heart, he lived on the rich man's estate and pretended to be the owner.

Upon taking hold of the estate, the dishonest servant fired anyone who knew the father or the son and hired a new staff. When the son returned several years later, no one remembered him except the family dog and the dishonest servant. The servant had the young man thrown off the estate, calling him a liar and a beggar. As in the case between the two women, the young man sought Solomon's judgment to have what was rightfully his restored to him.

A 17th century painting depicts Solomon hearing the case of the two mothers who each claim that a living child is theirs. In his collection of folklore Legends of the Jews, *the scholar Louis Ginzberg described Solomon's wealth and his wisdom. "Under Solomon's rule silver and gold were so abundant among the people that their utensils were made of them instead of the baser metals," wrote Ginzberg. Elsewhere in the book, Ginzberg noted, "But Solomon's wealth and pomp were as naught in comparison with his wisdom."*

Each man who claimed to be the rightful heir to the fortune filled a vessel with his own blood. Solomon dipped an arm bone taken from the old man's body into the blood of each and declared, "See! The blood of the son hath found the flesh of the father and cleaveth thereto, and they are become one. He it is who is the son of the dead!" The true son's blood stuck to the father's bones, and the disobedient servant's blood did not.

Solomon already knew the identity of the true heir because of the way the son reacted when he ordered that the father's grave be opened and his body desecrated to remove his arm. However, the experiment was necessary to prove the son's identity with certainty to the other witnesses present in the court. Here again, Solomon used his knowledge of familial love to determine the truth and ruled in favor of the young man.

SOLOMON'S WISDOM

When he became king, Solomon asked God to grant him understanding so that he might rule God's people fairly. These stories depict Solomon's wisdom after it was heightened by God's fulfillment of this wish. However, other stories illustrate Solomon's natural powers of deduction in childhood. One such story involved two shepherds on a journey and an egg. Having eaten all of his own food, one shepherd was still hungry.

The hungry traveler noticed that his companion had one hard-boiled egg left from his supper and asked his companion if he could have it to eat. The companion

Dating Solomon's Lifetime

Because of the scarcity of artifacts dating back to Solomon's time, it is difficult to create an exact time line of Solomon's life. This problem is compounded by differences in the Jewish and modern calendars and the scarcity of dates in the religious and historical accounts of Solomon's life. However, the following approximate dates can serve as a basic outline of King Solomon's life.

983 B.C.E.   Solomon is born to David and Bathsheba.
971 B.C.E.   David has Solomon proclaimed king of Israel, then dies.
960 B.C.E.   Building on the first temple in Jerusalem is completed.
943 B.C.E.   Solomon dies.

agreed to give it to him only under the condition that the egg should be considered a loan and not a gift. The hungry man agreed to repay his egg in full when the lender asked for it at a later date.

Some years passed, and the companion who had lent the egg returned to the once hungry shepherd to demand his payment. The lender explained that the borrower owed a large sum of money for all of the chickens and eggs the borrowed egg would have become during the time that had passed since the egg was eaten. Since the shepherd could not repay the amount the lender said he owed, both men went to the court of King David, Solomon's father. There, they requested that David hear and deliver a fair decision in their case. Though he felt sorry for the borrower and thought the deal was unfair, King David saw no other choice but to decide in favor of the lender because of the promise the borrower made when he ate the egg.

The child, Solomon, saw the man who lost the judgment on his way out of the court and decided to help him. Solomon instructed the man to take a pot of boiled beans into a field that his father and his soldiers would be passing the next day. When the soldiers were in view, the man was to plant the beans in the ground. The soldiers saw the man and found his behavior strange because boiled beans cannot produce plants. When they questioned him about his actions, the man responded as Solomon had instructed him, "Whoever saw boiled eggs hatching out chickens!" When King David heard about this from his soldiers, he knew who the man must be.

Because he was acquainted with the man from his court appearance, David also knew that he was not capable of planning this exhibition on his own. His suspicions that Solomon had given the shepherd instructions were confirmed when he questioned the shepherd who had been planting boiled beans in the field. King David reversed his original judgment and told the man he owed no more than one egg. At the end of the story, King David was a little angry with his son, but when Solomon explained the reasons behind his actions, David forgave him because he viewed him as a wise and compassionate child.

Legends such as these show Solomon not only as an extraordinarily wise man, but also as one who had compassion for his fellow man. This is not to say that Solomon was always without fault, however. From the descriptions provided of Solomon as an adult, it is clear that he made mistakes during his rule and throughout his adult life. Like all people, Solomon was sometimes ruled by his passions rather than his mind.

SOLOMON IN HIS OWN TIME

In his own time Solomon was famous for several reasons. He brought unity to the kingdom his father, David, had established, and accomplished large construction projects, including Jerusalem's first permanent temple. All of Israel shared the same faith, and because of that, the temple brought the people together by giving them a place they could look to as the center of their faith. Additionally, Solomon's wisdom brought wealth and prestige to Israel because leaders from foreign countries came to seek his advice. These leaders brought lavish gifts with them, which were used to fund building projects and fill Israel's coffers.

Perhaps Solomon's greatest accomplishment was to complete his father's work of uniting Israel's twelve tribes into a single kingdom. This unification enabled Solomon to fulfill his father's promise to build the temple, as well as to provide municipal services such as roads and irrigation to the people of Israel. These things did not come without a price, however. Solomon is often criticized for taxing his

Jewish men pray at the Western Wall, which is believed to have been part of a retaining wall built around the foundation of the Jewish Temple. Solomon's temple was constructed on a hill at this site that today is known as the Temple Mount.

Seeking Solomon's Wealth

Modern interest in stories and legends related to the wealth of King Solomon is readily visible in popular literature. To illustrate this fact, one need only type "King Solomon" in the search bar at Amazon.com or Google to receive a multitude of entries in a matter of seconds.

During the 19th century, British author H. Rider Haggard created one of the most memorable fictionalized quests for King Solomon's treasures. His Victorian novel *King Solomon's Mines* is an adventure story in which the hero, Allan Quatermain, and a band of explorers set off into the jungles of Africa in search of immeasurable wealth. In the novel Quatermain must not only overcome cultural and environmental barriers in his quest, but also outwit riddles and traps supposedly set by King Solomon in order to protect the ancient King's treasure. Several movies based on the novel have been made; it has also had a strong influence on the development of other film characters, such as Indiana Jones.

More recently, Sean Kingsley detailed his real-life adventures searching search for King Solomon's treasures in his 2007 book *God's Gold: a Quest for the Lost Temple Treasures of Jerusalem*. Tahir Shah detailed his own experiences looking in Ethiopia for the source of Solomon's wealth in his 2003 book *In Search of King Solomon's Mines*.

Interestingly, in October 2008 archaeologists reported the discovery of copper mines at Khirbat en-Nahas, in present-day Jordan, that may have been operated during Solomon's reign in the tenth century B.C.E.

Though Solomon's riches have captured the minds of men and women in much the same way as lost pirate gold and other buried treasures, Solomon's gold is not the only treasure future generations hope to gain from him. Steven K. Scott published *The Richest Man Who Ever Lived: King Solomon's Secrets to Success, Wealth, and Happiness* in 2006. In it Scott details what he believes is Solomon's greatest gift, the path to happiness.

people heavily in order to meet his goals for the fledgling state.

Solomon also enslaved non-Israelites living in the kingdom, forcing them to work on his building projects. The Bible says:

> All the people left from the Amorites, Hittites, Perizzites, Hivites and Jebusites (these peoples were not Israelites), that is, their descendants remaining in the land, whom the Israelites could not exterminate—these Solomon conscripted for his slave labor force, as it is to this day. But Solomon did not make slaves of any of the Israelites; they were his fighting men, his government officials, his officers, his captains, and the commanders of his chariots and charioteers. They were also the chief officials in charge of Solomon's projects—550 officials supervising the men who did the work. (1 Kings 9:20–23)

To modern readers, it may seem strange that the Israelites would have enslaved another people. After all, a few hundred years before the time of Solomon, the Israelites themselves had been slaves in Egypt. But to Solomon's contemporaries, the king's action in enslaving potential enemies would be seen as wise. It would ensure the continued rule of the Israelite people in the region while accomplishing Solomon's building goals at the same time.

SOLOMON IN HISTORY

Although King Solomon is revered as an important Israelite leader, he was not without flaws. In fact, it would be an injustice to portray him as a perfect, two-dimensional cardboard cutout. For members of those faiths who share Solomonic legends, only God is entirely good. Everyone else struggles with human faults and imperfection. It is only through an honest examination of Solomon as he is portrayed in the many legends and stories of his life that readers can gain an understanding of the way in which he used his gifts of wealth, power, and wisdom for the good of his people. It is this understanding that provides a basis for comparison between Solomon and modern leaders so that modern students can learn how Solomon's lessons can be used in today's societies.

THE RISE OF A MONARCHY

In order to understand the role Solomon played in the land of Israel, it is necessary first to understand what Israel was like before and during the time of David, Solomon's father. Biblical archaeologists Israel Finkelstein and Neil Asher Silberman make the reasons for understanding the relationship between David and Solomon, as well as the kingdom they built, clear when they write, "The story of David and Solomon's establishment of a powerful, prosperous United Monarchy of Israel has provided a model of righteous leadership enshrined in the Judeo-Christian tradition and in every society that has drawn its moral authority from it."

Modern leaders take cues from the leadership of Solomon. In order to understand his life and rule, however, it is important to understand his beginnings through a brief examination of David's life, since Solomon did not blaze a new path for him-

21

self but instead continued his father's work.

From the time of Moses, Israel was divided into 12 tribes. Although the tribes worked together and there was a man appointed king, each tribe was governed separately. A true monarchy did not come about until David's reign and was not perfected until the height of Solomon's reign. In considering the effects this type of government had in Israel, it is important to remember that the royal houses of both David and Solomon were prone to a love of excess, which eventually caused the fall of the monarchy in the generation after Solomon. The traditional system of government began to change shortly before David became the king of Israel.

DAVID, SHEPHERD AND KING

David was born in Bethlehem to a family of shepherds. But despite his humble beginnings, God had great plans for him. In David's youth Saul attempted to unify the Israelites and led them victoriously in many battles with neighboring countries. Though he successfully increased the size of the land called Israel, he failed in his attempts to unite the people.

David's rise to power followed an unlikely series of events. One day, while David was looking after his father's sheep, Goliath, a soldier from the opposing army, approached the armies of Israel and said, "Choose a man for yourselves, and let him come down to me. If he is able to fight with me and kill me, then we will be your servants; but if I prevail against him and kill him, then you shall be our servants and serve us" (1 Samuel 17:8–9). The Israelites were afraid because Goliath was a giant compared to their own size and carried impressive weapons and armor. Because of their fear, no one dared stand against him.

The Renaissance artist Michelangelo created his famous sculpture of David around 1504. The sculpture depicts the young Israelite at the time he agreed to battle the Philistine giant Goliath.

When David came to bring supplies to his brothers who were in the Israeli army, he heard the giant's battle cry. David said to his fellow countrymen, "For who is this uncircumcised Philistine, that he should defy the armies of the living God?" (1 Samuel 17:26). Though David was already favored by God and had been anointed as Israel's next ruler by the prophet Samuel, he had not yet gained the trust of the Israelites. Since no one else came forward to challenge the giant, David prepared to answer him on the battlefield.

King Saul heard of David's plans and approved of his desire to battle Goliath on behalf of his people. He honored him by giving him gifts of armor and weaponry, but because David was so weak, he could not lift them. He knew that his best defense against Goliath was the quickness given to him by his small size. He also knew that if he met the giant dressed as the king had prepared him, he would not be quick enough to save his own life. Therefore, David removed the gifts Saul had given him and met Goliath on the battlefield armed only with a shepherd's staff, a few stones, and a slingshot. Years of practice with his slingshot gave David excellent aim, and against all odds, he killed Goliath with one shot.

King Saul was overjoyed at David's victory. However, his feelings of elation did not last long. The King became consumed with jealousy, fear, and rage because the people of Israel praised David for his victory. No amount of music could calm him. Saul's feelings led him to plot ways to have David killed. David heard of the king's plans and

This detail from a 12th-century Catalan painting shows David preparing to cut off the head of the Philistine giant Goliath.

fled to escape his wrath. Saul led his armies in pursuit of David. During this time, David had the opportunity to kill Saul twice and did not. Throughout his flight, he had been gaining followers and had amassed his own makeshift army. However, when news of his mercy toward his tormentor reached the ears of Israel, David gained even more support from the people, who respected his brave deeds and generosity toward Saul despite Saul's intent to kill him. When King Saul and his sons died in battle, the people took up David as their new king.

David's original kingdom began at Hebron. He already had six wives at that time and gained more wives and concubines throughout his rule at Hebron. Then, through the prophets, God told David he should move his kingdom to Jerusalem. It was not until much later that David married Solomon's mother, Bathsheba.

Bathsheba was the wife of one of David's greatest and most loyal soldiers, Uriah. Though it is not clear whether Bathsheba shared in or encouraged David's desires, David's desire for her is clearly evident. King David attempted to conceal his affair by calling Uriah to return home. However, as Israel Finkelstein and Neil Asher Silberman note in their *David and Solomon: In Search of the Bible's Sacred Kings and the Roots of the Western Tradition* "all of his attempts to persuade the good soldier Uriah to sleep with his wife, Bathsheba (and thereby provide a cover for her adulterous pregnancy) fail." This failure compounded David's sin, because he then sought Uriah's death. Since David could not murder Uriah, he devised a plot in which he would surely be killed on the battlefield.

The affair between David and Bathsheba carried much heavier penalties in ancient Israel than it would in today's society. Whereas adulterous affairs involving public figures today can carry public humiliation with them, they seldom result in the professional ruin of the people involved. In the time of David, publication of the affair would have resulted in his political downfall. In addition, because the society lived under Mosaic Law, the penalty for adultery was death. The Jewish people were warned, "If man commits adultery with the wife of his neighbor,

Solomon's Mother

Bathsheba—alternately spelled Bath-shua in the ancestry provided in 1 Chronicles—is one of the most misunderstood women of the Bible. She is remembered as the mother of Solomon and the favored wife of David. In art, she is often presented as a seductive manipulator.

While there is no doubt that David desired her or that she accepted the king's advances, from the account of their affair presented in 2 Samuel, there is no suggestion that she intentionally attracted his attention. In fact, the only time she is shown manipulating the king is when, under the influence of David's advisor, she enters the king's bedchamber to remind David of his promise to make Solomon his successor as king.

Despite her blamelessness as depicted in the Old Testament stories of her, blame for David's attraction to her, the affair, and Uriah's death have for centuries come back to rest on Bathsheba in the minds of biblical commentators and laypeople alike. Bathsheba was certainly a powerful and influential woman as the favored wife of King David and later the Queen Mother in Solomon's reign. However, the sin that resulted in the dissolution of her first marriage was not hers, at least in its entirety. As a loyal subject, she could not refuse the king's invitation.

Solomon was not Bathsheba's only child. In addition to the first child born of her adulterous relationship with David, Bathsheba also bore three other children—Shimea, Shobab, and Nathan.

both the adulterer and the adulteress shall be put to death" (Leviticus 20:10). There is a second warning: "If a man is found lying with the wife of another man, both of them shall die, the man who lay with the woman, and the woman; so shall you purge the evil from Israel" (Deuteronomy 22:22). The seriousness of this type of offense is clear from both the harshness of the penalty prescribed and the double mention of it in Mosaic Law.

As a devout man of faith, David would most assuredly have known of these prohibitions. Therefore, when his attempt to hide his sin failed, he was left with few options. David sent Bathsheba's unsuspecting husband to the front lines of battle so that he would be killed. After a short mourning period, David and Bathsheba were married, but their happiness could not be complete. David's secret, though not made public, was no longer entirely private. Nathan, the king's prophet, brought news to David that God was displeased, and though God forgave David, the sin had to be punished. The child conceived in adultery died as a punishment for his parents' sins. God did not communicate directly with David, but through prophets. Therefore, Nathan, the prophet who brought David the news of God's disappointment, was made aware of the king's sin. Because of the seriousness of adultery under Mosaic Law, Nathan's knowledge gave him power over the king, and David had to be careful of Nathan for the remainder of his life.

God's anger toward David was short-lived, and he was granted a son—"Then David comforted his wife Bathshe'ba, and went in to her, and lay with her; and she bore a son, and he called his name Solomon. And the Lord loved him, and sent a message by Nathan the prophet; so he called his name Jedidiah, because of the Lord" (2 Samuel 12:24). The name Jedidiah means "beloved of

God," and the name Solomon means "peace." Thus, from his birth Solomon acted as a favored peace offering between God and David. During his rule Solomon's name took on a greater significance as he brought peace and diplomacy to the land of Israel.

THE PEACE BEARER

Traditional religious texts provide little information regarding Solomon's childhood and early life. The chronicler of the Old Testament, for instance, provides only that Solomon was very young when he ascended his father's throne. Likewise, texts such as Hayyim Nahman Bialik's *And It Came to Pass: Legends and Stories About King David and King Solomon* provide only a few stories of Solomon's youth that tell of his innate gifts of wisdom and justice. Clues outside of Solomon's story presented in 1 Kings pertaining to other kings' sons shed some light on what Solomon's early life might have been like.

As one of the king's sons, Solomon would have remained in the care of nurses inside the harem during his early years. When he was of age, Solomon's care would have been transferred into the hands of the best tutors so that he could receive instruction in the ways of the world and of his faith. If he was like his brothers, he would have married young and been given land by the king. He might also have been provided with cattle or some other way of generating income by his father. Though he would no longer have lived in the king's household at this point, he would still have been supported by the king and subject to him.

From other chronological clues provided in the Old Testament, biblical scholars typically infer that Solomon would have been approximately 12 years old when he became the king of Israel, but could have been as old as

20. Certainly by modern standards, this age seems extremely young for a ruler. However, from the accounts of other men provided in the Old Testament, this age would have been an appropriate time for Solomon to marry and leave the royal household. Since he was made king, he took control of the royal household instead of leaving it.

Furthermore, historically, youth has not been an impediment to assuming the throne. For instance, Tutankhamen became pharaoh of Egypt when he was seven years old, and ruled until his death around the age of 18. Likewise, James II of Scotland was just under seven years old when he became king in 1437 C.E., and Louis, king of the Franks, was only 6 years old when he ascended the throne in 899 C.E. From a historical standpoint then, it is not surprising that Solomon should have gained the throne at an early age in approximately 970 B.C.E.

However, since David and Bathsheba were married later in David's life, it is surprising that Solomon, a child of that union, should become king, rather than one of David's older sons from previous marriages. In fact, two of Solomon's half brothers attempted to take the kingdom before David appointed Solomon as his successor. During this early period of the monarchy, there was not a right of succession as it existed during later European monarchies.

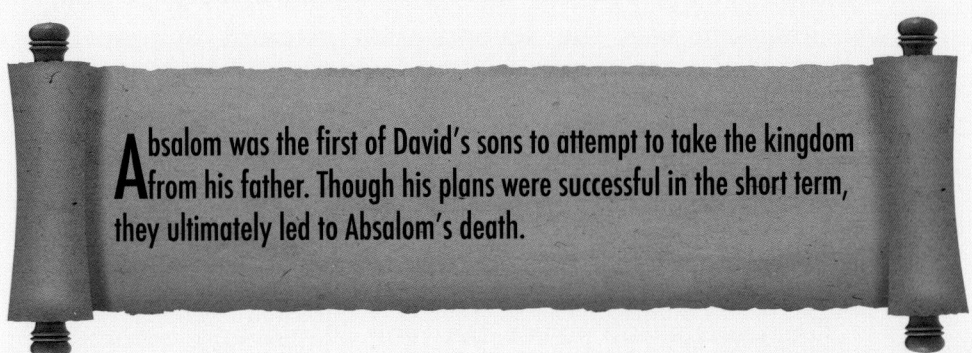

Absalom was the first of David's sons to attempt to take the kingdom from his father. Though his plans were successful in the short term, they ultimately led to Absalom's death.

Most often, the kingdom was passed to the person who found favor with both the Israelites and their God, as was the case with King David. Conversely, Solomon's fate was sealed by a promise made to his mother. Bathsheba reminded David of this promise when Adonijah (one of David's other sons) attempted to make himself king.

While he was on his deathbed, Bathsheba went into her husband's room and said: "My lord, you swore to your maidservant by the Lord your God, saying, 'Solomon your son shall reign after me, and he shall sit upon my throne.' And now, behold Adonijah is king, although you, my lord the king, do not know it" (I Kings 1:17–18). Because he was ill, David had been removed from the affairs of his kingdom and had no knowledge of Adonijah's plans to take over the kingdom. When he heard this news, which was almost immediately confirmed by Nathan, one of the king's closest advisers, David ordered that a ceremony should be held immediately in which Solomon would replace David as the ruling monarch.

Solomon was anointed by both Nathan, the prophet, and Ado, the priest. Loud trumpet blasts and festive music were heard throughout the land, and all the people joined in the refrain, "Long live King Solomon" (1 Kings 1:39). It was not usual either in David's time or in later monarchies for a son's accession to happen before the ruling monarch's death. However, Adonijah's attempt to take the kingdom was the second such attempt by one of David's sons. Furthermore, Adonijah's success would mean the death of both Solomon and Bathsheba because Adonijah would perceive them as threats to his newly acquired kingdom. Therefore, David acted in the only way available to him to protect the lives of Solomon and Bathsheba while fulfilling his promise to Bathsheba.

The transfer of power between David and Solomon

Illustration from a late 13th century Bible depicting Bathsheba speaking with the aged King David, and the king's selection of Solomon as his successor.

provided David with peace in his final days. Upon hearing the news of Solomon's accession, David thanked God, saying: "Blessed be the Lord, the God of Israel, who has granted one of my offspring to sit on my throne this day, my own eyes seeing it" (1 Kings 1:48). David trusted in his son's wisdom and faithfulness. Because of this, David told Solomon of the things he felt he had left undone during his reign and abandoned his affairs into the hands of his young son. Though he fulfilled the final wishes of his father early in his reign, Solomon did not trust in his own wisdom.

While David still lived, Solomon ruled the kingdom as his father had. As a young man and a new leader, Solomon had much to learn. He did not have complete confidence in himself and sought right judgment above all else in order to govern his people fairly. Thus, Solomon found solace and council in the familiar faces of his father's court. Those who were faithful to David remained faithful to Solomon as God's next chosen king for Israel. Likewise, those who were threats to David and his kingdom remained so under the new rule. Solomon knew that it was imperative for him act quickly in carrying out his father's final wishes so that he could establish himself as a competent and confident leader for the country.

Not long after Solomon's accession, David died, leaving Israel completely in Solomon's hands. Because he was faithful to his word and obedient to his father, Solomon lost no time in removing those his father had seen as threats to the kingdom. Some of David's unfinished business involved death as punishment for treason or other past crimes. Solomon was not a warrior as his father had been, and it was important that his hands stay clean so that he could fulfill another of his father's wishes and his promise to God by building a permanent dwelling place for the Lord among the people. Therefore, Solomon sent Benaiah, who was David's, and now Solomon's, chief bodyguard, to carry out death sentences.

Once Solomon's promises to his father, with the exception of building the Temple, were complete, he was able to begin building his own kingdom. At once Solomon married, began naming captains from his trusted advisors, and delegated responsibilities to them. However, to Solomon, faithfulness and wisdom were the most important parts of becoming a successful ruler. With that in mind, Solomon prayed that God would grant him a spirit of understanding.

AN ENLIGHTENED AGE

Peace, diplomacy, and learning were highly valued during Solomon's reign. These provide the greatest examples for modern leaders to follow. "The biblical story of David and Solomon is not just a standard work of self-serving royal propaganda," assert Israel Finkelstein and Neil Asher Silberman. "It was—and is—a passionate and sophisticated defense of Davidic legitimacy, powerful enough to be argued in the public squares or meeting places to still the voices of criticism with the skill of its argument and its considerable narrative art." In both the way it is told in the surviving ancient texts and in its characteristics, Solomon's reign exemplifies a golden age in the history of the Israelites and acts as a model to which all leaders since can aspire.

According to the Bible, King Solomon's reign lasted for 40 years. Because of the roundness and symbolic nature of this number, scholars often debate its accuracy. However, since to date very little archaeological or other historical evidence exists to refute this time frame, the number remains the accepted starting point for discussions relating to the Solomonic period. Regardless of the actual duration of Solomon's reign, Finkelstein and Silberman affirm "The biblical description of King Solomon's forty-year reign of royal prosperity and grandeur (1 Kings 3–10) has provided western civilization with some of its most glittering images of enlightened kingship, guided by wisdom and blessed with unparalleled wealth. With a regal bearing unmarred by David's violent

The Significance of 40

In the Bible, certain numbers are considered to have particular importance. One of these is the number 40, which occurs numerous times in both the Hebrew Bible and the New Testaments. For example, in the story of Noah, it rains for 40 days and 40 nights. In Exodus, the Israelites wander in the desert for 40 years. In the New Testament, Jesus fasts in the Wilderness for 40 days (Mark 1:13; Matthew 4:1–11; Luke 4:1–13). In these instances, the time period represented by 40 is a time of testing or trial, followed by a period of renewal.

In other books of the Bible, 40 is used to denote a long period in Israel's history as a nation. Often, this is a prosperous time because of a good ruler. In the book of Judges, the Israelites enjoy peace during the 40-year reigns of Othniel, Barak, and Gideon. David's rule lasts for 40 years, as does Solomon's.

Some scholars contend that in the Bible, the number 40 simply represents a long period of time—possibly the length of a generation. Others contend that the number is used accurately, and is a sign of God's consistency. All agree, however, that the many examples of 40 in the Bible have great spiritual importance.

background and warrior image, Solomon serenely establishes an efficient bureaucracy to administer his vast kingdom and presides over a court and palace that is renowned for its opulence and refinement."

In order to establish this new kind of court that would become the model for future generations, Solomon had to establish new kinds of relationships both inside and outside the Israelite kingdom.

It should be remembered that neither Solomon nor the kingdom he ruled was perfect. Though he cared for the Israelites and provided them with many good things, he was also prone to excesses that would ruin him and, eventually, his kingdom. It is important to examine the good that came about during Solomon's reign and his unification of the people in Jerusalem. These things brought peace to a region whose history up until that point had been marked by unrest. To accomplish this goal, Solomon had to employ the use of new diplomatic methods as well as his gifts of wisdom and understanding.

THE QUEST FOR KNOWLEDGE: GOD'S PROMISE

Soon after David's death, Solomon began his reign in earnest and fulfilled the promises he made to his father concerning unfinished business. During that time of transition, Solomon received a prophetic dream, one of the earliest forms of prophecy recorded in the Hebrew culture. In the dream, God came to Solomon and asked what Solomon desired either for himself or for his kingdom. Solomon replied:

> You have shown great and merciful love to your servant David my father, because he walked before you in faithfulness, in righteousness, and in uprightness of heart toward you; and you have kept for him this great and merciful love, and have

given him a son to sit on the throne this day. And now, O Lord, you have made your servant king in place of David my father, although I am but a little child; I do not know how to go out or come in. And your servant is in the midst of your people whom you have chosen, a great people, that cannot be numbered or counted for multitude. Give your servant therefore an understanding mind to govern your people, that I may discern between good and evil; for who is able to govern this great people of yours? (1 Kings 2:6–9)

God was pleased with Solomon's request both because of the way in which Solomon addressed him in his prayer and because the request was an unselfish one. While Solomon could have asked for anything, he asked only for the wisdom to be able to tell right from wrong so that he could be a fair and just ruler to the people. Therefore, God promised Solomon wealth and a long life in addition to unsurpassed wisdom. God's promises were conditional, however. Solomon did not possess perfect wisdom, since he was human and perfection of any kind is reserved for divinity. Wisdom and the other gifts God promised Solomon would only be his if he obeyed God's commands closely.

While folktales and various religious traditions sometimes contradict one another as to when Solomon received the gift of wisdom, they seem to agree on two things. First, that Solomon was extremely wise. Second, that to whatever degree he possessed this gift before his vision, Solomon's wisdom increased greatly because he found special favor with God and was loyal to God's teachings.

For many traditions, God's favor also leads to other gifts, such as the ability to control the wind, animals, and

Illustration titled "The Wisdom of Solomon" and depicting the king judging the claims of the two mothers, from the Book of Hours of Louis d'Orleans, *an illuminated manuscript on vellum, ca. 1490.*

demons. The Qur'an mentions jinn, demons, and the winds submitting to the power granted Solomon. Other books also refer to Muslim traditions and folktales regarding King Solomon. For example, there are no stories about Solomon in *One Thousand and One Arabian Nights,* the famous collection of stories from the Middle East. However, several stories in the collection refer to his great power and wealth.

Solomon's newfound powers were constantly tested. In several tales Solomon is tested by lesser creatures. For example, upon being told that God had granted dominion over all creatures to a human being, one bird protested because the king would be lower than his subjects if the

An illustration from an 1895 edition of the story collection One Thousand and One Nights, *also known in the West as* The Arabian Nights. *Although none of the stories are specifically about Solomon, he is referred to numerous times in the collection. For example, in the story of Sinbad the Sailor, the main character gives a ring engraved with Solomon's seal to the Islamic caliph, Harun al-Rashid.*

birds that obviously fly over the king's head were to be subject to Solomon's rule. The bird said:

> The eagle alone is our king. He ever reigned and
> ever will reign! Him alone hath God set high above
> all winged creatures: therefore he flieth highest
> and dwelleth highest above all.

Solomon, who now could understand the language of the birds and all other creatures, recognized wisdom in the little bird's statement. In order to prove that he was indeed ruler over all the creatures of the earth by God's command, Solomon commanded all of the birds within hearing to come to him. In the presence of all those gathered, he gave the little bird a task. He tied a letter around the bird's neck and told her to deliver it to the chief eagle. The letter read, "I, Solomon, son of David, King of Israel, bid thee, O aged king, saying, Hasten forthwith and come unto me!" When the king of the birds arrived and humbly submitted to King Solomon, he rode on the eagle's back. He commanded the bird to come back on an assigned day each month. When the bird returned, Solomon again mounted its back and flew wherever he wanted to go.

Solomon proved his dominion over the birds through this gesture. In similar stories he did likewise to frogs, lions, bees, and demons by taming the greatest of each of these creatures. By speaking languages unknown to other humans, Solomon also solidified his control over the people of Israel because these things showed his great understanding of the natural world and his willingness to listen to even the least among his subjects. While Solomon could have used powers such as these for his own glory, he chose to use them for the good of his people and the glory of God for the duration of most of his reign.

Since all people did not possess Solomon's insight, others often lacked the vision to find the wisdom in his decisions and prescribed courses of action. Thus, when Solomon sent the princess of Aram, Keziah, to live in an unapproachable tower until her future husband should find her, she and her father both wept bitterly. Solomon argued that God had a plan for each person and that God's plan would find the person regardless of the obstacles standing in its way. Though his plan to lock the maiden in a tower seemed perfectly logical to him because his trust in God was so great, it seemed like madness to others around him.

Eventually, a young man who had been shipwrecked and almost drowned in the sea found the princess. He was brought to the deserted island by a giant eagle. The island's only inhabitant was the lonely princess in the tower King Solomon had designed. The eagle was the same one upon which Solomon rode every month and brought the princess's daily food rations under Solomon's orders. When love found the princess despite all of the difficulties put into place, others were able to see Solomon's wisdom in the truth he had spoken.

Great leaders often take risks that seem foolish to others. Though unnecessary risks are always unwise, sometimes, for those with complete understanding of the situation, clarity of vision minimizes the risk involved. Wisdom necessitates a thorough understanding of a given situation and the realization that decisions and courses of action have an effect on others beyond those intimately involved in the situation.

Occasionally, Solomon would forget that the power and wisdom granted him was not his, but was a gift granted to him by God. On these occasions, he would use the power for his own good, rather than that of his people.

Though wars were not fought during Solomon's reign, the people of Israel were forced to endure hardships when their king had lapses in judgment or bouts of willfulness. Both the people and the king had to repent and make sacrifices in order to restore the kingdom's glory in these situations.

Eventually, the pride and unrepentant spirit from which Solomon sometimes suffered led to the kingdom's downfall. For the most part, however, Solomon's reign provided a time of peace, security, diplomacy, wealth, and advancement for the people of Israel.

SOLOMON'S ROYAL HOUSEHOLD

Though the king's mother held special privileges beyond those granted to the queen in ancient Israel, a queen was a necessary part of the royal household. She held two important functions. The first was to provide heirs to the king in order to continue the royal lineage. The second was to act as a symbol to the people and keep them united in case the king was drawn away in battle. Though God promised David that Solomon's reign would be a peaceful one, the people would not necessarily have known of that promise. Thus, it was important for Solomon to marry quickly in order to start his reign on a solid foundation in the perception of his people.

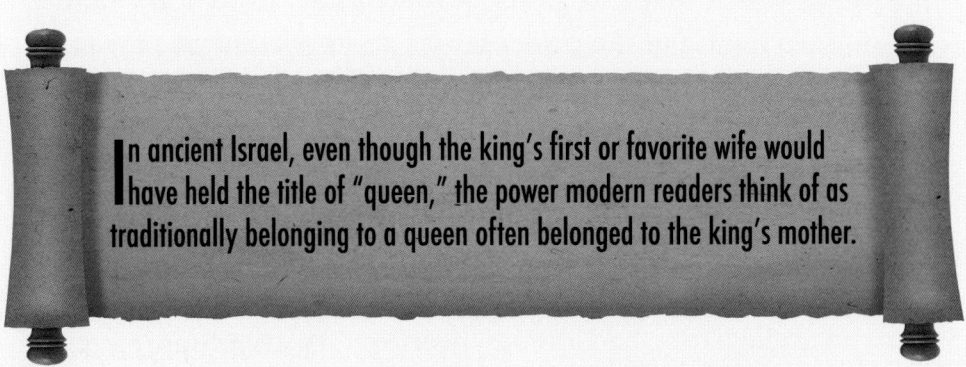

In ancient Israel, even though the king's first or favorite wife would have held the title of "queen," the power modern readers think of as traditionally belonging to a queen often belonged to the king's mother.

In ancient Israel marriage customs and, indeed, the social institution of marriage itself differed greatly from modern concepts and traditions. However, it was not very different from marriages elsewhere during the same period. Whereas today men and women enjoy many of the same rights and privileges in most parts of the world, the same was not true in Solomon's time. Women were regarded as property in the ancient world. For the most part they were not trained in trades; women were taught by their mothers how to manage a household, but would not be able to provide for themselves outside of the home. As possessions of their fathers, young women could be traded in marriage for political or social reasons and then became possessions belonging to their husbands.

While polygamy was allowed, it was not common among the middle and lower classes because the practice was expensive. Women needed to be cared for and maintained like any possession, so acquiring many wives or concubines was an expensive venture. If a man possessed enough resources, he could obtain numerous wives and concubines. By making alliances through these marriages, a man could strengthen his influence in domestic or foreign affairs.

According to the Hebrew Bible, Solomon's first wife was the daughter of the Egyptian pharaoh. At that time, Egypt was a major regional power. Thus, Solomon's marriage to the Egyptian princess was an important one for the Israelites. This marriage cemented political and diplomatic ties between Solomon's Israel and Egypt. It might not have been possible had Solomon already been married. The Pharaoh's daughter would have been a great prize. Knowing this, it would have been unlikely that the Egyptian ruler would allow his daughter to marry a king whose allegiance had already been split by other marriages.

With this alliance, Solomon solidified his place in the Near East and forged bonds of friendship between Israel and Egypt. This friendship extended to encompass Phoenicia, because that country was largely under Egyptian control and influence at the time. This relationship would have increased trade and encouraged peace between the countries. Since both Egypt and Phoenicia were centers of learning, the alliance would also have

The Great Sphinx and pyramid at Giza, Egypt. The kingdom of Israel held a critical position between two major centers of ancient civilization: Egypt and Mesopotamia. Historians have speculated that Israel prospered under David and Solomon because the nascent nation was able to control the trade routes between these two centers of power.

increased the perception that Israel was a place where intellectual pursuits were prized and cultivated.

Interestingly, Solomon's wives and concubines remain nameless in traditional texts, but their nationalities are well documented. Traditionally, Israelites married other Israelites to preserve their faith. Thus, Solomon's tendency to marry outside of Israel is another marked departure from the status quo of his time. Some evidence exists that this trend carried over into the lives of commoners so that

The Royal Harem

The word *harem* refers to the group of women who were married to or were concubines of the king. The practice of maintaining a harem was common among kings in the ancient Middle East. Solomon's harem was not unique to him in any regard other than the number of women in his harem.

The word *harem* can also refer to the building or part of the royal palace where these women lived. The king's children came from the relationships the king had with women inside his harem. However, a king would not necessarily have intimate relationships with all of the women.

Kings often married to forge diplomatic relationships for the good of their countries. Thus, because of his country's relationship with other countries, a king might not always have been able freely to choose the women who would be part of his harem.

Furthermore, the king inherited his father's harem. While he may have had relations with some of the women from his father's harem once they became part of his own, this does not mean that the king took all of his father's wives and concubines into his bed. Since there were not many ways for a woman to support herself outside of marriage, the widows and children left behind when a king died needed someone to take care of them.

they too began to see marriages between themselves and outsiders as acceptable.

As king, Solomon's monetary and other resources were indeed great. His harem reflected this with numbers almost inconceivable to the modern mind. When discussing the harems of other kings in the region, Roland de Vaux writes, "But all these are eclipsed by the fabulous harem of Solomon." Solomon's excess in this matter is clearly spelled out in the Hebrew Bible: "He had seven hundred wives, princesses, and three hundred concubines" (1 Kings 11:3). While this many women would increase the king's progeny, such a large household would make it extremely difficult for Solomon to fulfill his promise of faithfulness to God, concentrate on matters of state, and lead his people properly.

Solomon would not have chosen all of his wives and concubines. De Vaux explains, "From some passages, it appears that the king's harem, at least in the early days of the monarchy, used to pass to his successor." This provides an explanation for one of the most perplexing conversations in the Biblical account of Solomon's life.

When Adonijah, Solomon's half brother, wanted to make David's nurse, Abishag, his wife, he sought the council of Bathsheba. His conversation with Solomon's mother and the way in which she was received by the king support the arguments that the king's mother was granted special influence and privileges in ancient Israel and that the king's harem passed to his successor. That Adonijah sought Bathsheba's aid in obtaining his desire is not surprising in the light of this knowledge. What is surprising to modern readers is the way in which Solomon answered this request.

When Bathsheba entered her son's throne room, he bestowed great honor upon her by having her seated on a throne next to him. He promised to listen to and grant whatever request she brought before him. However, when Bathsheba asked that Abishag, David's nurse, become Adonijah's wife, Solomon became enraged and swore, "God do so to me and more also if this word does not cost Adonijah his life! Now therefore as the Lord lives, who has established me, and placed me on the throne of David my father, and who has made me a house, as he promised, Adonijah shall be put to death this day" (1 Kings 2:23–24).

Solomon's response to Adonijah's and Bathsheba's request seems like an overreaction. Yet if, as de Vaux suggests, the king's harem went to his successor, the reasons behind King Solomon's anger are clear. Years earlier, when David's son Absalom rebelled and forced David from the throne, he went into his father's house and lay with David's concubines. This was a key moment in Absalom's victory, proving that he had defeated David and claimed his royal perogatives. Thus, since Solomon already knew that Adonijah had supporters from his previous plot to overthrow the crown, his brother's request for a member of Solomon's harem was an act of treason and therefore punishable by death.

Having preserved his harem, thereby securing his throne, Solomon faced the prospect of having to provide for such a large family. With Solomon, over 300 concubines, 700 wives, plus the offspring and household servants, the needs of the royal house were indeed great. In order to meet the needs of his family, Solomon formed the largest cabinet of advisors in Israelite history up to that point. He then charged each of these with fulfilling the royal household's needs from their own storehouses for a period of one month.

THE DAWN
OF DIPLOMACY

Israel enjoyed peace and prospered under Solomon's rule. In order to provide for his family and help secure peace throughout the kingdom, Solomon enlisted the aid of 12 officers, according to the Hebrew Bible. Their names were Ben-hur, Ben-de'ker, Ben-he'sed, Ben-abin'abab, Ba'ana (the son of Ahi'lud), Ben-ge'ber, Ahin'abab, Ahi'ma-az, Ba'ana (the son of Hu'shai), Jehosh'aphat, Shim'e-i, and Geber. Many of the men listed were the sons of those who fought with and defended David. Others were married to Solomon's daughters. From this list, it seems clear that Solomon would have appointed these men over the length of his reign rather than at the beginning, because when he first became king, Solomon would not have had daughters old enough to be married. Therefore, he would have had no sons-in-law at the beginning of his reign.

Another officer is listed separately from the others, and only by his region. This was the captain from Judah. Though officially within the boundaries of Solomon's kingdom, Judah had always been considered a land apart. Judah had been David's power base, enabling him to unite the tribes of Israel under his rule. Consequently, both David and Solomon treated Judah differently than the other tribes.

All of Solomon's officers were allowed to govern their regions with little interference from the king. They also enjoyed prestige among the people and wealth gained from their regions.

One of the responsibilities of each officer was providing the necessary food and horses for the royal household for one month out of each year: "And those officers supplied provisions for King Solomon, and for all who came to King Solomon's table, each one in his month; they let nothing be lacking. Barley also and straw for the horses and swift steeds they brought to the place where it was required, each according to his charge" (1 Kings 4:27–28). These provisions were to come from each officer's storehouses, which were filled from the region in which each officer lived. Each month contained 29 to 30 days.

THE 13 PROVINCES

In the Bible, the number 12 is significant. It is symbolic of the original 12 tribes of Israel. However, Solomon divided his kingdom into 13 regions, rather than 12, so they do not correspond exactly to the ancient tribal territories.

The addition of a 13th officer is confusing at first, because it seems that the Deuteronomist's count is inaccurate. However, it is quickly explained with a brief look at the Hebrew calendar and the region this officer governed. Though the needs of the providing officer's own house would have been included in the needs of the royal house, since he dined at the king's table during his month,

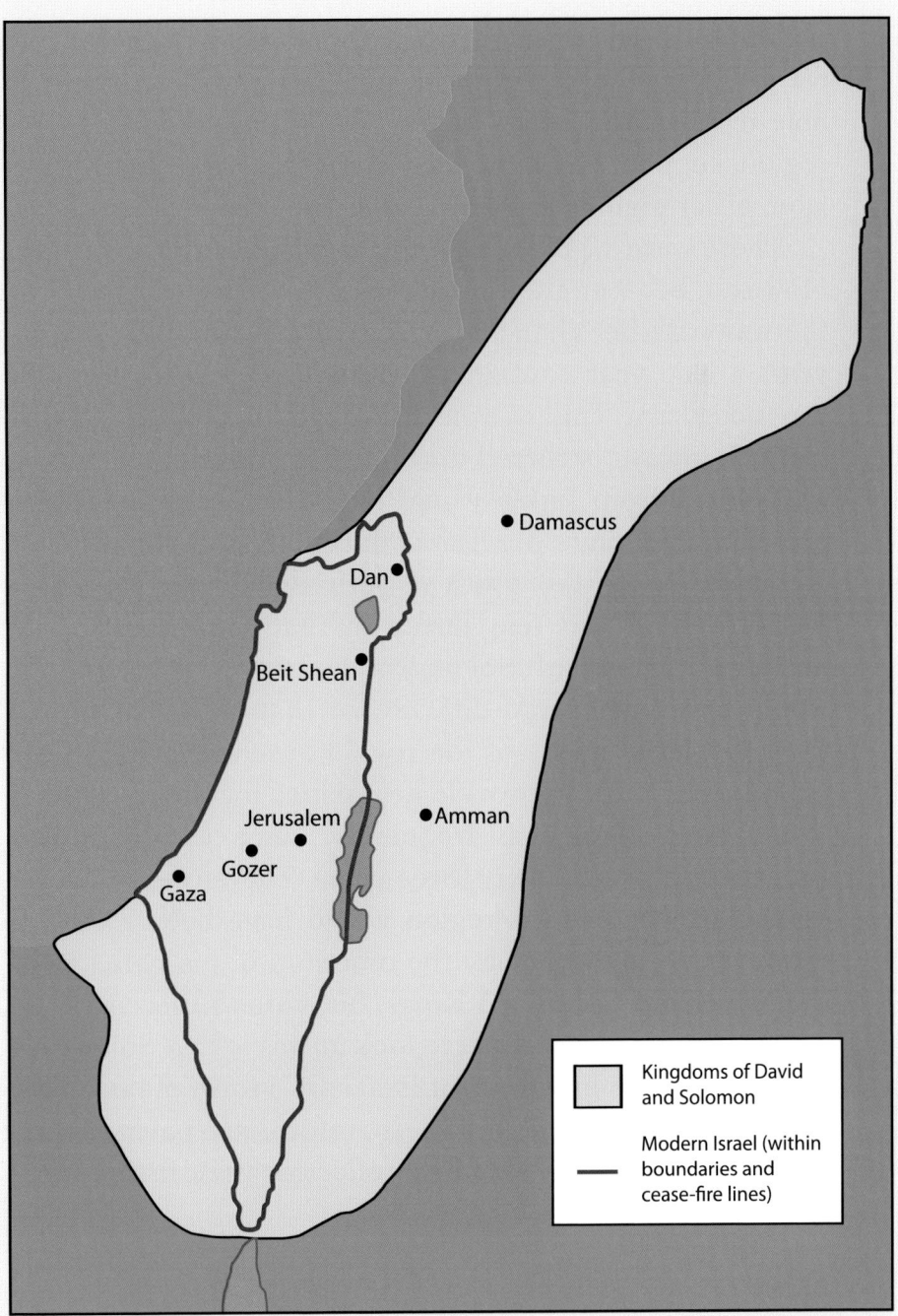

In Solomon's time, the kingdom of Israel stretched from the Sinai desert to the Euphrates River and from the Mediterranean Sea to the mountains east of the Jordan River. It encompassed parts of present-day Lebanon, Syria, Iraq, Jordan, and Egypt.

Solomon's needs were great and would have been difficult for a less profitable region to meet. If an officer was not able to meet the needs of the royal house from his own region, supplies to fill the king's table had to be brought in from other regions at great cost to the responsible officer.

There were 12 months in the regular Hebrew calendar. However, because the calendar was based on the cycles of the moon rather than the cycles of the sun, every three years a leap year containing an additional 29-day month was necessary. This was necessary to ensure that Jewish festivals always occurred during their prescribed seasons. The officer from Judah would have been responsible for providing the king's provisions during this odd month.

Judah lies to the south of Jerusalem, near the Dead Sea. The land was less fertile in that area than in the northern regions of Solomon's kingdom. Therefore, it would have been more difficult for that region to supply the substantial needs of the royal household. The officer from Judah's turn to provide necessities for the royal table would have come less frequently, since the leap year occurred only once every three years. Therefore, the drain on this officer and his region would have been reduced. However, as is evident by the omission of his name from the record presented in 1 Kings, his status suffered.

Of course, another way to look at this is that Solomon's demands on the provinces of Israel are a form of tax on his people. The people of Judah, therefore, are paying lower taxes than the other Israelites, reflecting their favored status in the eyes of the king.

SUPPLYING THE ROYAL HOUSEHOLD

The basic needs of Solomon's royal house are clearly spelled out in the Old Testament: "Solomon's provision for one day was thirty cors of fine flour, and sixty cors of meal, ten fat oxen, and twenty pasture-fed cattle, a hundred sheep, besides deer, gazelles, roebucks, and fattened fowl" (1 Kings 4:22). Modern readers of this passage understand that the quantities listed are large, but they have difficulty forming a picture of just how large these quantities were. For example, unless someone is familiar with the modern meatpacking industry or cattle farming, he or she probably has no idea how much meat one cow or one sheep would provide. The standard of measurement used for flour and meal in the passage, *cor*, is also problematic to modern readers because it is no longer used.

Opinions differ as to the actual size of a cor. In some versions of the Bible, the word is translated as "measure." Other ancient references suggest that a cor as it is used here is the same as a homer, or one donkey-load, but again those measurements are difficult to understand because they have no real meaning in modern society. The cor was a unit of measurement for volume, like the modern bushel. Estimates suggest that one cor translates to six and one-quarter bushels.

The two types of flour would not have been used together, since each is used to make different kinds of bread. Meal is a coarser grain and was used for making common or everyday bread. Fine flour was normally reserved for honored

Solomon required enormous amounts of wheat and other foodstuffs to maintain his household.

guests and royalty. However, since both were used in making bread for the daily meal, it is helpful to combine the quantities needed of each in order to understand the amounts listed in this passage. Thirty cors of fine flour plus 60 cors of meal yields 90 total cors. That is about 562.5 bushels. By converting bushels to cups, the measure turns into about 2,343 cups. That is enough to fill 293 five-pound bags of flour like the ones found in supermarkets today. It would weigh approximately 1,465 pounds, or three-fourths of an American ton. That is enough to make about 5,000 loaves of bread each day, depending on the recipe used.

Solomon, his household, and guests did not dine on bread alone, however. The passage also mentions oxen, cattle, sheep, and game. Two types of cattle are listed. Oxen would have been raised and fed with grain in narrow stables, while the cattle mentioned would have grazed in pastures. Since the cattle were allowed to get at least some

A shepherd walks with his herd in modern-day Israel. In the ancient world of the Bible, ownership of livestock represented great wealth.

exercise, they would have been smaller and produced leaner meat.

Since the amount of game is not specified, it is difficult to estimate how much the household consumed. However, since the amount of cattle and sheep needed each day is listed, and because these animals are still consumed today, the quantities can be estimated. An average cow weighs about 1,200 pounds, and an average sheep weighs about 150 to 200 pounds. Both animals yield about half their weight in usable meat. That means Solomon's daily portion of sheep meat would have been about 1,000 pounds, and his daily portion of beef would have been about 15,000 pounds.

Using the average modern weights of cattle and sheep would mean that over the course of a 30-day month, Solomon's household required 240 tons, or 480,000 pounds, of meat in addition to immeasurable amounts of wild game. However, it is possible that cattle and sheep would have been smaller in ancient Israel. Even if the animals were half the size of today's animals, Solomon's household would consume about 120 tons in a 30-day period. In modern-day America, Solomon's daily rations would feed between 16,000 and 32,000 people per day.

Solomon's captains were not only to provide the food for his table, but also food for his horses, as well as for additional horses when the king needed them. Since Solomon had 40,000 horses, feeding them was no easy task. Today, an average 1,000-pound horse would need about two pounds of barley and 20 pounds of hay each day. Thus, if they were all of average size, Solomon's horses would require 800,000 pounds of hay and 80,000 pounds of barley each day.

When the biblical proportions are converted to modern-day measurements, it is easy to see how much each of Solomon's captains needed to provide to the king's household in order to hold their privileged positions. These portions had to be provided and prepared daily.

The cost of these supplies is difficult to determine for two reasons. Modern equivalents for the standard ancient measures provided in 1 Kings are not exact. Monetary conversions are similar. However, modern cost estimates based on the figures given earlier provide a good idea of what Solomon's daily provisions would cost in today's markets. In the United States, flour costs approximately $3.50 per five-pound bag. Coarser ground meal costs about $2.00 per pound. Beef and sheep meat prices vary greatly depending upon the age of the animal and the cut of meat used. Sheep can cost from 89 cents per pound for less desirable cuts to $100.00 per pound. Beef prices vary in the same way, but for the sake of estimating the costs of Solomon's daily provisions, the averages of $10.00 per pound for sheep, $5.00 per pound for beef, and $2.75 for flour will be used. Using these prices, Solomon's daily rations would cost approximately $85,805.

In 2009, the minimum wage for workers in the United States was raised to $7.25 per hour. If a person earning that wage worked a regular 40-hour work week, it would take that person almost six years to pay for one day's food rations for Solomon's household. If all of the animals needed for one day's ration, plus those needed to carry flour and meal, stood in a single file line, they would stretch across four football fields, including the end zones. When looking at these figures, it is important to remember that the amount of money needed to provide horses, hay, barley, and game are not included in these estimates, so the cost would be even greater.

Since news of Solomon's wisdom traveled widely in the region, the court was often filled with guests. The daily

An ornate copy of the Qur'an, the holy book of Islam. In their book David and Solomon: In Search of the Bible's Sacred Kings and the Roots of the Western Tradition, *Israel Finkelstein and Neil Asher Silberman describe how Solomon's reputation as a great leader was adopted into the growing Muslim empire during the seventh and eighth centuries* C.E. *"As Islam spread through the Near East, North Africa, and the Balkans, the image of David and Solomon also exerted a lasting impact in the consciousness of caliphs, sultans, and imams," they write. "The Qur'an had adopted a great deal from the biblical tradition and both Daoud and Suleiman appear in the Islamic lore as noble kings and judges who precociously expressed the will of Allah. Suleiman, in particular, was regarded as one of the four greatest leaders in history, along with Nimrod, Nebuchadnezzar, and Alexander the Great."*

rations provided in these passages would also have been used to feed any visitors to the court. Such a plentiful array of food would no doubt have been useful in impressing the kingdom's guests in addition to feeding them.

ISRAEL'S REPUTATION AMONG THE NATIONS

During Solomon's reign, Israel enjoyed great prestige among its neighbors. "The stories of Solomon in the Bible are uniquely cosmopolitan," write Israel Finkelstein and Neil Asher Silberman. "Foreign leaders are not enemies to be conquered or tyrants to be suffered; they are equals with whom to deal politely, if cleverly, to achieve commercial success." The merchant class prospered during Solomon's reign because international and regional trade flourished. Since Solomon's reign was peaceful, an open dialogue between the leaders of various countries was encouraged. Both of these factors enabled Israel in general, and Jerusalem in particular, to grow in wealth, culture, and learning. This growth made Israel into a cosmopolitan power that rivaled Egypt and Phoenicia.

Because of Solomon's wisdom and Israel's success during his reign, legends of Solomon spread beyond the borders of Jewish traditions into Islam and eventually to the far reaches of Africa. This ensured that Solomon and his kingdom would have a lasting impact on the annals of history.

One of Solomon's best-known visitors was the Queen of Sheba. The country of Sheba existed in the southernmost part of Arabia about 1,000 miles from Solomon's kingdom. About the time Solomon reigned, Sheba conquered the country now known as Ethiopia on the continent of Africa. Though Ethiopia is now a third-world country and suffers from great poverty, during Solomon's time it was a source of riches. Because of the riches in Ethiopia, the resources of Sheba's other colonies, and those present in Sheba, the Queen of Sheba and her people were a wealthy nation.

The Queen's visit to King Solomon is mentioned in all of the religious texts that tell his story. The stories differ in the way in which she came to him and the particulars of her visit. Some stories suggest that she came to Solomon on her own after hearing of Solomon's great wisdom, while other legends claim that the she came to Solomon after receiving a letter from the king.

The stories and legends agree on three things. The first is that Solomon passed whatever tests the Queen brought before him. Secondly, the Queen brought great riches, including gold, silver, and spices, with her from her kingdom as gifts to give King Solomon if he could pass her tests. Finally, the Shebites worshipped the sun instead of the Hebrew God and were converted to Judaism because of the Queen's experiences in Israel. For instance, the Old Testament notes: "And when the queen of Sheba had seen all the wisdom of Solomon, the house that he had built, the food of his table, the seating of his officials, and the attendance of his servants, their clothing, his cupbearers, and his burnt offerings which he offered at the house of

The Queen of Sheba

The Queen of Sheba is shrouded in mystery. She is most famous for her visit to King Solomon sometime in the 10th century B.C.E., but little else is known about her. Even the exact location of her country is unknown to modern scholars. Most suggest Sheba is where modern day Yemen is located, but others claim that her kingdom was in Africa, in what is now Ethiopia. The compromise is the assumption that Ethiopia was a territory of Sheba, which was where Yemen is today.

Speculation is plentiful regarding the relationship between Solomon and the Queen of Sheba. Some traditions claim that the two had a romantic relationship that resulted in a son who eventually became the king of Ethiopia. Since no documented historical accounts of the queen's visit exist from the 10th century B.C.E., religious texts and folktales must be the primary sources for any examination of their relationship.

The 17th century Flemish artist Frans Francken the Younger created this painting of the Queen of Sheba kneeling before Solomon. According to the Jewish
scholar Louis Ginzberg, who collected stories and folktales about figures from
the Bible in a multi-volume work titled Legends of the Jews, when the queen
meets Solomon she attempts to test whether he is as wise as is rumored.
Ginzberg writes, "Then the queen began and said: 'I have heard of thee and thy
wisdom; if now I inquire of thee concerning a matter, wilt thou answer me?' He
replied: 'The Lord giveth wisdom, out of His mouth cometh knowledge and
understanding.'" The queen proposes numerous riddles, which Solomon answers
unerringly, Ginzberg notes. "Then she said to him: 'Thou exceedest in wisdom
and goodness the fame which I heard, blessed be thy God!'"

the Lord, there was no more spirit in her" (1 Kings 10:4–5). Here, as in other legends, Solomon answers all of the Queen's questions and challenges so that she believes all the tales she has heard about him and comes to believe in God as a result.

One legend from the Jewish tradition explains how the Queen of Sheba set out to test the king's wisdom and senses. After testing the king with several riddles, she filled a large room with thousands of artificial flowers of all kinds. Then, she placed one single real flower among them. The artificial flowers were of such a good quality that they looked exactly like their real counterparts in nature. The queen brought King Solomon into the room and asked him to pick out the real flower from among the fake ones.

Since Solomon spoke the language and understood the ways of all living creatures, he opened the door and called a bee into the room. Though all of the flowers looked real, the bee quickly found the genuine flower among all of the others because it could smell what human noses could not. Solomon's tactics seem tricky, but since the queen did not place any limitations on how he was to find the real flower, she accepted his method as an exhibition of his wisdom and as proof that the God of Israel was the true God, since it was God who gave Solomon the gift of wisdom.

SOLOMON AND THE DEMONS

Solomon's gifts exceeded his wisdom. The Qur'an mentions Solomon's power over the winds several times. This passage, in particular, names the other gifts Solomon gained from God: "And We subjected the wind to Solomon, blowing in the morning the space of a month and in the evening the space of a month; and We smelted for him the fount of brass. Of the jinn some worked before him, by the Leave of his Lord, and whoever of them served from Our Command, We shall make him taste the punishment of the blazing Fire" (Qur'an 22:34). Though the Qur'an uses the pronoun we, in this passage and in others like it, the pronoun should be understood as the royal we. Only one God exists in Islam. According to this passage, God gave Solomon power over the jinn, also known as genies. The jinn are beings made of smoke and light. In some instances, and in other religious traditions, they are called demons.

The passage also mentions Solomon's control over the winds. This is illustrated in several stories in which Solomon and others ride atop a magic carpet or cape. Though those who do not understand the powers given to Solomon would call the carpet magic, Solomon only used the carpet as a way for the wind to carry him. It was not the carpet that he commanded, but the wind instead.

In some instances it appears that the winds and demons under Solomon's control were one and the same. For instance, when Solomon was building his Temple to the God of Israel, he received a letter from the king of the Arabians, Adares. The letter told of a strange wind that was plaguing the Arabians. For days it had killed people and animals because it blew so fiercely. Adares begged Solomon, "Forasmuch as the spirit is a wind, contrive something according to the wisdom given in thee by the Lord thy God, and deign to send a man able to capture it." Solomon heard the distressed monarch's plea, and in seven days he sent one of his servants to capture the wind.

The people of Arabia did not believe that Solomon's young servant would be able to put an end to their torment, because all of their bravest men had already tried to quiet the wind and failed. However, the young man followed King Solomon's instructions precisely. He sealed the demon that had been causing the terrible wind into a flask and closed the top with the king's seal. Since God had given Solomon's seal special power to chain and force even the fiercest demon to obey, the demon captured in the flask was unable to escape. After waiting three days to make sure the Arabian people would not be tormented any longer, the young servant began his trip back to Solomon with the flask. When he returned, Solomon released the demon from the flask. He instructed it to lift a stone that had been too heavy for the other human and demon builders of the Temple to move. When it was at the desired height, Solomon bound the demon again with his seal so that it had to support the weight of the stone for as long as the Temple stood, or until Solomon decided to release it.

RULING WISELY

Through the powers given to Solomon by God, Solomon was able to impress the leaders of foreign countries. He combined his knowledge of the natural world with his power over demonic forces and cleverness resulting from his gift of wisdom in order to solve the problems of other leaders and successfully pass their tests. With this, he was able to improve not only his own reputation among the people of those countries, but that of Israel as well.

Solomon brought stability to Israel and the region surrounding it throughout his 40-year reign. Israel Finkelstein and Neil Asher Silberman point to this in their book when they write, "Solomon's image promises security, stability, and happiness in a world in which boundaries are fluid and national glory is achieved through wisdom and commercial acumen." By using his gifts to gain the trust of his own people and that of foreign leaders,

Solomon was able to improve his country's reputation. Solomon's diplomatic efforts solidified these relationships, as did Solomon's marriages to the daughters of neighboring countries. These marriages and relationships also resulted in the expansion of Israel's borders.

Growth is certainly good. However, Solomon's marriages produced an extremely large household that had to be fed and supplied. Additionally, the country's growth placed an increasing burden on Solomon as king. By dividing his kingdom into sections, each under the government of one of his captains and advisors, Solomon was able to ensure that his household's needs were met. At the same time, Solomon lessened the burden of government upon his own shoulders with these appointments because he filled the positions with men he trusted.

BUILDING
THE KINGDOM

I srael's increased stability led to more commercial trading with its neighbors. With that, the wealth of the merchant class increased. Thus, Solomon's captains were able to collect enough in resources and taxes to supply his needs. This greater wealth and stability brought greater unity to the kingdom and allowed King Solomon to build several buildings for public and private use.

Solomon built several structures for his own use, but even these lent prestige to Israel. One example of such a building is Solomon's massive royal palace. It put all palaces before it, even David's, to shame because of its size and grandeur. F. W. Farrar says of David's palaces and household, "But his harem and his palaces were insignificant compared with those of Solomon, who in his splendour and magnificence followed the dubious model of Egyptian, Phoenician, and Assyrian kings."

Farrar suggests that Solomon's opulence in creating his palace and his large harem was excessive. Indeed, throughout history, these have provided some of the reasons for Solomon's downfall.

While it is easy to see Solomon's excess in hindsight, his people enjoyed the fame he brought to Israel and did not seem to mind his overindulgence until near the end of his reign. Even those buildings whose sole purpose was to serve the king brought glory to Israel and increased its reputation of culture and wealth among its neighbors in Solomon's heyday. Of all the construction projects Solomon completed during his rule, the Temple in Jerusalem is his most famous.

During the time of Moses, God gave directions that an ark and a moveable tabernacle in which the ark would be housed should be constructed. Both the ark and tabernacle had been built and filled according to the

The Israelites carry the Ark of the Covenant across the Jordan River. Detail from a Christian mosaic made in Rome during the fifth century C.E.

specifications God set forth. The ark contained a jar of manna, the food God provided for the Israelites during their long flight to freedom from Egypt. The stone tablets with the commandments given to Moses written on them, and the staff of Aaron, which God had made sprout overnight, were also included in the ark. Through time it became known as the Ark of the Covenant, because it contained items to remind the Israelites of the promises made by them to God, God's promises to them, and the familial bond they entered because of these promises.

All of these items were to serve as reminders to the Israelites of God's goodness and greatness. Though the people knew of the contents, once these were enclosed in the ark and the ark was placed inside the tabernacle, only priests were allowed in the inner chamber of the tabernacle and then, only once each year. This was because God chose this as his dwelling place among the people, and only those who had been sufficiently purified could stand in God's presence. Once each year, the high priest would enter the inner chamber and receive instructions from God for the people of Israel.

When the tabernacle and the ark inside were built, the Israelites were nomads in the desert searching for the land God had promised them. They would carry these items with them and reconstruct the portable tabernacle when they reached the place where they would set up camp for the night. However, the ark was not always meant to be moveable. The poles by which it was carried were to be removed when the Israelites reached the Promised Land. There, they would erect a permanent dwelling place for God.

King David wanted to build God's Temple in Jerusalem, but was unable to accomplish this. God promised David that one of his sons would be made King after him and that the son would have the privilege of constructing the Temple. David began pooling resources for this construction during his reign and instructed Solomon to build it when he became the king of Israel.

THE TEMPLE OF SOLOMON

The specifications of Solomon's Temple are outlined clearly in the Old Testament in much the same way as the daily provisions for his royal family were:

> The house which Solomon built for the Lord was sixty cubits long, twenty cubits wide, and thirty cubits high. The vestibule in front of the nave of the house was twenty cubits long, equal to the width of the house, and ten cubits deep in front of the house. And he made for the house windows with recessed frames. He also built a structure against the wall of the house running round the walls of the house, both the nave and the inner sanctuary; and he made side chambers all around. The lowest story was five cubits broad, the middle one was six cubits broad, and the third was seven cubits broad; for around the outside of the house he made offsets on the wall in order that the supporting beams should not be inserted into the walls of the house. (1 Kings 6:2–6)

Solomon's Temple probably still existed at the time the Deuteronomist captured its image in words. The detail with which he describes the outside of the Temple illustrates its importance to the Israelites. For modern readers, this description is difficult to understand for the same reason Solomon's daily food rations are difficult to understand. The measurements used in the Old Testament are unlike those used in the modern day. However, with a few conversions, this description is easily deciphered.

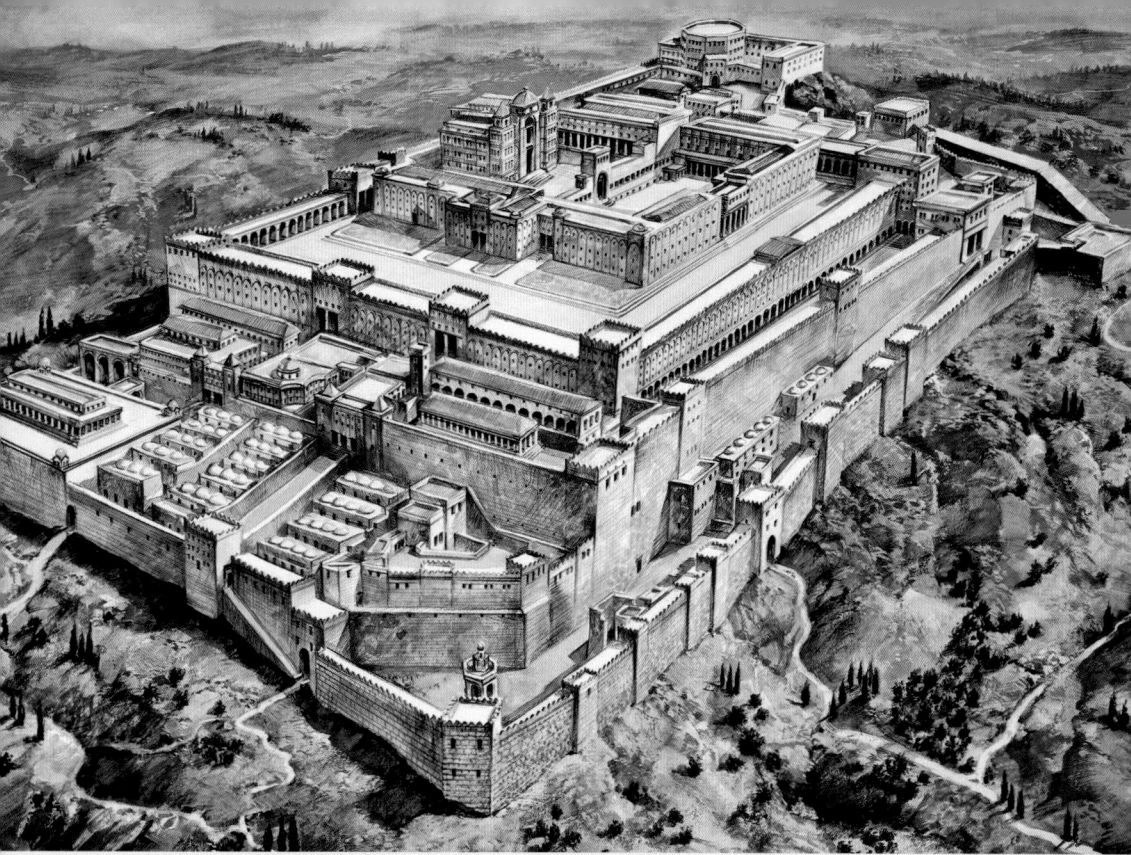

This illustration, based on the Biblical description and archaeological evidence, shows how the temple in Jerusalem may have appeared.

Sean Kingsley explains, "The cubit traditionally measured the length of a man's forearm, from his elbow to his clenched fist, and was the principle unit of linear measurement in the Bible." Since Solomon was the king, the cubit referred to in this passage would be the royal cubit, which was just a little longer than its ordinary counterpart. Generally, this is a little more than 1.7 feet. Using these measurements, the main body of Solomon's Temple including the vestibule would measure about 120 feet long by 34 feet wide, or a little less than one acre.

Its shape was a long, narrow rectangle. If 12 tractor trailers were lined up end to end and side by side, they would be roughly the same size and shape as Solomon's finished Temple. Three trailers side by side would make up the width, and four trailers end to end would make up the length. The main part of the Temple was as tall as it was wide.

The building was divided into three sections, as the portable tabernacle before it had been. From front to back, these were the vestibule, the sanctuary, and the inner sanctuary. The ark was kept in the inner sanctuary, the most holy of all places. The level of purification required as the priests approached the inner sanctuary increased, just as it had with the Tabernacle in Moses's day.

The entire building was built atop a platform with shorter storage chambers surrounding the building on three sides. No storage rooms were located at the end of the building used as an entrance. These rooms were accessible from the inside of the Temple. It is likely that they contained treasures brought to the king from the leaders of other countries and nonperishable offerings of great value brought to the priests from visitors to the Temple.

The Temple's ornaments and furnishings are described in the Old Testament in great detail as well. All of the materials used for the construction of both the inside and outside of the Temple, as well as the Temple's furnishings, were the best of their kind. Solomon used cedar and cypress trees from Lebanon to make the walls on the inside of the Temple and the roof because of their strength and their ability to resist decay. The distance from Lebanon to Jerusalem is about 150 miles. With today's transportation methods, this is not a great distance, but in Solomon's day, the journey would have been difficult and would have taken about one month to complete. Olive wood was used for the creation of the inner doors and statues of cherubim within the Temple because of its beauty.

On the inside of the Temple, Solomon had the wood and stones decorated with intricate carvings of religious symbols. The beams and floors were overlaid with gold because of its beauty and value. No expense was to be spared in creating the Lord's house. All of the stones and timber from the trees were prepared elsewhere "so that neither hammer nor axe nor any tool of iron was heard in the Temple while it was being built" (1 Kings 6:7). This was an amazing feat, since the stones and timbers would have been extremely heavy, and their preparation needed to be precise to ensure that they would fit into their proper places at the building site.

For the Temple adornments and furnishings, Solomon adhered to the specifications God had given and commissioned the creation of those items required by God. These

Idolatry in the Temple?

Biblical descriptions of the ornate decorations inside Solomon's Temple and surrounding the structures outside of the Temple are filled with images of animals, fruits, and other elements of the natural world. Some have seen these as symbols that Solomon worshipped other gods and thus created graven images like the one of the golden calf the people of Moses created. Even the ancient Jewish historian Flavius Josephus suggested that Solomon may have sinned by including these images in the Temple's decor. However, a closer examination of these images reveals that they are meant to be symbols to aid the faithful in their worship. These are but a few of the symbols used in the Temple and their meanings:

Object	Meaning
Pomegranates	Good works
Cherubim	Divine presence
Eagles and lions	Royalty and dominion over the earth
Oxen	Hard work

were things such as pillars, large basins so the priests could purify themselves and the people's offerings, pots, shovels, and lamp stands. Most of these items were cast out of bronze, an expensive metal in Solomon's time. The items used in the innermost section of the Temple were made from pure gold, an even more expensive metal. Such a massive undertaking required the use of many skilled craftspeople and thousands of laborers.

According to accounts of the Temple's construction in the Qur'an and Kabbalah, men were not the only workers forced into labor to build Solomon's Temple. The Qur'an mentions devils "who dived for him and did other work besides" (Qur'an 17:21). The jinn too were enlisted in Solomon's service "to fashion for him whatever he wished of palaces, statues, basins like water-troughs and immovable cooking pots" (Qur'an 22:34). From these passages, it is evident that Solomon had spiritual help in completing the Temple and his other building projects. What is not evident from the passages is the exact manner in which these beings were made to help Solomon or how he was able to control them.

The kabbalistic text known as the Testament of Solomon explains these things well. In it, Solomon tells how he was given a ring that had a seal on its top in the shape of a pentagram by the archangel Michael. The angel came as an answer to Solomon's prayer, in which Solomon had begged God for control over a demon who was distressing one of his favorite workers so he could deliver the boy from the demon's grasp.

After praying all night, Solomon was visited by the angel, who gave him the ring and said:

> Take, O Solomon, king, son of David, the gift
> which the Lord God has sent thee, the highest

Sabaoth. With it thou shalt lock up all the demons of the earth, male and female; and with their help thou shalt build up Jerusalem. But thou must wear this seal of God.

The ring enabled Solomon to see and understand the demons brought before him and protected him from their powers. With it, he was also able to summon and bind the demons, so they were forced to do what he ordered them to do. The remainder of the text names the demons in Solomon's service individually, explains how each could be overcome, and details the work he or she performed in building the Temple.

At the end of seven years, the Temple was complete. Though not the same shape, the Temple would have had approximately the same square footage as a modern-day superstore. With modern equipment and laborers, Solomon's Temple would have required less labor and would have been completed in less than one year's time. Of course, it would also not have been built from such fine materials.

After the Temple was complete, Solomon held a dedication ceremony. All who were able to attend came to the dedication to praise God and to see Solomon's magnificent Temple. The ark was carried throughout Jerusalem until it finally came to its resting place inside the Temple. Israel was filled with a spirit of great joy. The celebration and feast that accompanied it lasted for a period of seven days, one for each of the years spent constructing the Temple.

When the week had passed, the people were sent back to their homes. Up until this point, Solomon had spent his life watching his father amass supplies for the building of the Temple, collecting these supplies himself, and finally,

Solomon offers a prayer at the dedication of the temple. The Jewish scholar Louis Ginzberg noted, "Among the great achievements of Solomon first place must be assigned to the superb Temple built by him. . . .

"Every detail of the equipment and ornamentation of the Temple testifies to Solomon's rare wisdom. . . .

"It was Solomon's meritorious work in connection with the Temple that saved him from being reckoned by the sages as one of the impious kings, among whom his later actions might properly have put him."

constructing the Temple. Now that the work was finished, Solomon was left without a project to occupy his time. Though he had finished the Lord's house, the king still did not have a house of his own. It was with that motivation Solomon began the construction of his own palace. Solomon's palace took 17 years to complete, more than double the amount of time spent on building the Temple and its furnishings.

SOLOMON'S PALACE AND OTHER CONSTRUCTION PROJECTS

Solomon began work on his palace adjacent to the Temple as soon as the Temple was finished. In 20 years, both were complete, which means Solomon spent 13 years building his own dwelling and only 7 building God's. However, as

F.W. Farrar noticed, "Kings that have once indulged their passion for magnificence by the erection of great buildings are scarcely ever content with rearing a single edifice. Solomon's work as a builder was continued with more or less activity through the remainder of his reign." Having successfully completed work on the Temple and thereby fulfilling a promise made by the Israelite people to their God and the promise Solomon made to his father, Solomon set out to find new construction projects. With that motivation, he began building up the rest of Jerusalem and continued into other parts of his kingdom.

Though Solomon completed many other construction projects in his lifetime, his throne is the most impressive. It was second in grandeur only to the Temple. According to legend, its complexities have yet to be duplicated. As in Solomon's construction of the Temple, only the finest materials were used.

The throne itself was made of ivory and covered in gold. Jewels of all kinds sparkled from it, and Solomon's headrest was covered in the softest lambs' wool so that he would be comfortable while presiding over the cases brought before him. The seat was then placed at the top of six steps.

Hayyim Nahman Bialik provides an excellent description of King Solomon's throne in his collection of legends and stories. Eagles and lions outlined the sides of the steps leading to the throne. "On each of the six steps of the throne were six lions of gold and six eagles of gold, on this side and on that, lion facing eagle, and eagle facing lion, the right paw of every golden lion facing the left wing of every golden eagle." These animals represented Solomon's kingship. The eagle was seen as the ruler of all the animals in the sky, and the lion as the ruler of all the animals on the earth.

Solomon's throne would have been impressive if this completed its construction. However, other animals joined the eagles and lions on either side of the steps that led up to the throne. Bialik continues, "On the lowest step lay a lion of gold with a bullock of gold opposite to it; on the next step was a wolf of gold with a lamb of gold opposite to it; on the third, a leopard of gold and a kid of gold; on the fourth, a bear of gold and a gazelle of gold; on the fifth, an eagle of gold and a dove of gold; and on the sixth, a hawk of gold and a sparrow of gold; while perched on the top of the throne was a great golden dove having a golden hawk caught within its claws." In the natural world, these animal parings would not exist, because they are all natural enemies. However, since Solomon was a fair and just judge with authority over human and animal affairs, the animals were able to coexist peacefully.

When Solomon would ascend his throne, he did not walk up the steps. Instead, the animals facing each other would support him on one of their paws or wings and raise him to the next set of outstretched paws. This was made even more fantastic by a giant eagle that swooped down to place Solomon's crown upon his head and a silver dragon that circled Solomon once he was seated on the throne.

Though made of gold, the animals would come to life and speak Solomon's praises when he made a decision in the court. If someone in the court lied, the animals would again come to life, causing a cacophony with their bleating, chirping, and other animal noises. Visitors to the court were awed by this display and proclaimed Solomon's greatness and the greatness of the God he served.

After Solomon's death, when Israel was once again torn apart by wars, Solomon's throne came into the hands of Israel's enemies. The throne's magnificence was legendary by that time. Though it passed into the hands of several different conquerors and all tried to mount it, the lions would allow no one but King Solomon to sit on the throne. Like many of the other things of Solomon's era, it was lost to time.

Solomon's palace and the adjoining Temple doubled Jerusalem's original size. Because of this growth, the city's walls were in desperate need of restructuring. Thus, King

King Solomon seated on his throne, from a 15th century French manuscript.

Solomon increased the stability of the country by strengthening the city's walls. He refortified the walls of Jerusalem and extended them to include the Temple and his palace. He also had a new tunnel dug to bring more water into the growing city. The process Solomon used is outlined in *The Oxford Guide to People and Places of the Bible*: "The Jebusite water-shaft was retained for use in military emergencies, but Solomon dug a tunnel from Gihon along the edge of the hill. Sluice gates at intervals facilitated irrigation of the King's Garden in the Kidron Valley." With this new tunnel, Solomon was able to supply the royal gardens and the new Temple with water. During his reign, Solomon also developed the cities of Megiddo, Gezer, and Hazor by building new roads and storehouses in those cities.

Despite the historical account of Solomon's building projects in religious texts, very little of the actual structures remain. Over the last 200 years or so, archaeology has become an important way for modern societies to study the past. The search for evidence of Solomon's palace, throne, or the original Temple has turned up little to date. Archaeologists believe they may have found pieces of the Gates of Solomon that once marked the perimeter of Jerusalem. Stables that could have been part of those Solomon used to house his 40,000 horses have also been found. Some evidence supporting the existence of a monarchy ruled by Solomon has also been found in cities outside of Jerusalem.

However, clear evidence that items found within Jerusalem belonged to Solomon or that they were built during the time he reigned has yet to be found. A large part of the problem has to do with the way in which Jerusalem was built. Many archaeologists now believe "that each successive city built on the site of Jerusalem demolished the foundations and robbed previous levels of their stones, making it unlikely that archaeologists would find a great deal of these earlier structures." If, over the centuries, more modern structures in Jerusalem were built over existing ones, pieces of early structures would be inaccessible to archaeologists.

Most likely, the stones from the foundations of early structures would also have been reused in making new structures. This means that pieces of original buildings may not be where they once were according to the historical accounts written about them. It also means that dating archaeological evidence becomes next to impossible. This is compounded by the fact that the original site of Solomon's famed Temple and palace are located in a place that is sacred to Muslims, Jews, and Christians. Because of this, a proper excavation of the area cannot be conducted.

Despite a lack of historical evidence to support King Solomon's construction projects, these undertakings would have been extremely important to Solomon's people. Since, as Carol Meyers describes in her article, "Kinship and Kingship," "they contribute to the royal administration of national territory, while also signifying the power of the king," these structures would have supported King Solomon's authority to rule. Additionally, the Temple would have held special meaning to the people of Israel as a symbol of their faith. By placing it in the center of the capital city, Solomon ensured that Jerusalem would be seen as a spiritual center for the people of Israel. The royal palace's place next to this spiritual center would remind the people that Solomon's rule was ordained by God so that they would be less likely to rebel against him.

FALL FROM GRACE

As a well-known proverb says, all good things must come to an end. Israel's golden age as it existed under Solomon proved the truth of this statement. The peace, prosperity, and unity of Israel's united monarchy came to an end with that of its famous leader. Humans are by nature imperfect beings. Unfortunately, a person's shortcomings or failings rarely ever impact only the person possessing them. Solomon's flaws affected his family and his country.

King Solomon governed Israel from an early age until he died 40 years later. Toward the end of his reign, he became consumed with selfish pursuits. Though he honored God with lavish gifts for the Temple, he gave only a small percentage of what he himself possessed. He drank out of golden cups and surrounded himself with luxuries of every kind. Solomon did all of this at the expense of his people. Whether his captains acted in their capacity as advisors to the king is unclear. However, his failure to yield God's repeated warnings, the diversity of his harem, and the company he kept would suggest that if his advisors had spoken against his actions, he would not have listened at this point in his life.

Solomon's unrestrained extravagance was exemplified by the lavish decorations of his throne, the size of his palace, his enormous harem, and the daily food rations he required to support his household and guests. His palace was a complex of several halls, each having a specific purpose. It was larger than the Temple and took almost double the amount of time to construct.

God supplied Solomon with everything he asked for and more during his life. Despite his unparalleled wisdom, however, it seems Solomon was unable to recognize the value of these gifts. The resources he expended in pursuit of his own happiness suggests that, at least toward the end of his life, Solomon held himself in higher esteem than he held his God. The Qur'an warns against this spirit and the trouble it can bring. In the Qur'an, God says, "Work thankfully, O David's House; for few of My servants are truly thankful" (Qur'an 22:34). Through his ungratefulness and faithlessness, Solomon lost all that he had been given.

That Solomon sinned was not new. Both David and Saul sinned against God and were punished. Saul's kingdom was taken from him and he died in battle because of his wrongdoings. The people of Israel were punished, and David's child died for his sins.

However, the sins of the three kings, their attitudes toward their offenses, and their punishments differed significantly. Solomon's sins were many, and his punishment was a combination of those given to David and Saul. What was new was the way in which Solomon sinned and that he lost the love of the people in addition to God's favor.

SINS OF THE FATHERS: SAUL AND DAVID

God chose Saul to rule over Israel when they cried out for a king to look after them. Before that, the country was ruled by 12 judges, each of whom governed one of the 12 tribes of Israel. The people were no longer happy with their system of government and said, "We will have a king over us that we may also be like all the nations, and that our king may govern us and go out before us and fight our battles" (1 Samuel 8:19–20). King Saul was appointed to do as the people wished. Through the prophet Samuel, God told Saul that he was to conquer Israel's enemies. While he was engaged in these pursuits, God was happy with him, but then he made three mistakes.

Only the prophet or priest was allowed to make sacrifices on behalf of the people, but Saul grew impatient waiting for Samuel. He offered sacrifices in Samuel's place. Then, when he was battling the Philistines, he told the people they could not eat until he had defeated all of his enemies. Here, Saul's wording was important. He did not ask the people to fast so that he might achieve victory over their enemies or over God's enemies. Instead, he told them that under penalty of death, no one was allowed to eat anything until he vanquished his enemies. In both of these instances, Saul made himself like God.

Finally, he committed his most serious sin. Saul disobeyed a direct order from God. God instructed Saul through Samuel: "Now go and strike Am'alek, and utterly destroy all that they have; do not spare them, but kill both man and woman, infant and suckling, ox and sheep, camel and donkey" (1 Samuel 15:3). Saul thought better of the plan that was laid out before him. Instead of doing exactly as he had been instructed, he killed everyone except the king of the Amalekites and saved the best of their animals.

When Samuel learned what the king had done, he told Saul that God had turned his back on him and would find a new king for the Israelites. Saul admitted his sin and repented, but Samuel said, "I will not return with you; for you have rejected the word of the Lord, and the Lord has rejected you from being king over Israel" (1 Samuel 15:26). Though Samuel changed his mind and went with the king to help him worship, God did not relent and chose David as the next king over Israel.

Saul's sins were prideful. He allowed the power that had been given him to overtake him so that in his mind, he was justified in disobeying God's laws. His refusal to destroy Israel's enemies eventually brought more danger to the country. A child who survived Saul's armies allowed his hatred of Israel to strengthen as he grew older. Eventually, his descendants came to seek vengeance and attempted to destroy Israel in the time of Queen Esther.

This page from a 10th century manuscript depicts Solomon's father David playing a lyre. Although David was a sinful man, he always gave God a central place in his life. Thus the Bible describes David as "a man after God's own heart" (1 Samuel 13:14).

David's sins, on the other hand, were not prideful. Instead, they were the result of human failings. These were discussed in much detail earlier and so do not need much discussion here. David was overcome by his desire for Bathsheba and then had her husband killed to hide his carelessness. While these things did not go unpunished, God forgave David.

Since both leaders admitted their wrongdoings and sought forgiveness, the question arises as to why one was allowed to retain his kingdom and live while the other died after his kingdom was taken from him. The answer waits in Solomon's reign.

In his love for his wives, Solomon abandoned his faith in God. He obtained large sums of gold, silver, and other treasures at the expense of his people. Then, in an effort to increase respect for Israel among the other nations and make it like them, he led the Israelites away from their culture. Finally, he passed these shortcomings along to his sons, including the one who would be the next king of Israel.

His punishment differed from his predecessors because his kingdom was taken from his descendants but not from him. Solomon's son, Rehoboam, did not die as David's first child from his union with Bathsheba had. However, he was forced to flee Jerusalem in exile. Although he was allowed to rule over Judah for a short while, Israel lost all of the greatness that David and Solomon had instilled in it under Rehoboam's rule.

God provided Israel's leaders with a list of things they should not do. Solomon disobeyed all of these. The list of God's prohibitions to the kings of Israel is clearly set forth in the book of Deuteronomy: "Only he must not multiply horses for himself, or cause the people to return to Egypt in order to multiply horses, since the Lord has said to you,

'You shall never return that way again.' And he shall not multiply wives for himself, lest his heart turn away; nor shall he greatly multiply for himself silver and gold" (Deuteronomy 17:16–17).

Any promises made between a king and God would be added to these basic tenants. For Solomon, the only thing God asked in exchange for great wealth, stability, peace, a long life, and wisdom was faithfulness to his commandments. This sounds like a bargain that could be easily kept. However, Israel Finkelstein and Neil Asher Silberman describe Solomon's story succinctly when they write: "It is a vivid lesson about how the religious faithlessness of a luxury-loving leader can destroy a golden age." With great power and wealth often comes great pride.

MARRIAGE AND SOLOMON'S DOWNFALL

Solomon's excesses violated his promise to God. At the end of Solomon's story in the Old Testament, only one breach is listed: "For when Solomon was old his wives turned away his heart after other gods; and his heart was not wholly true to the Lord his God, as was the heart of David his father" (1 Kings 11:4). Even with the Temple of the Lord in his own backyard, Solomon pursued gods other than his own.

Polygamy and jealousy travel hand in hand. With over 700 wives and 300 concubines, it is no surprise that Solomon's affections would be torn between his wives or that he would be consumed with their concerns. Relationships necessitate compromise. Surely, with that many people under his roof, at least 200 of them felt slighted on any one day. It was probably in an effort to appease his wives and bring peace to his house that Solomon strayed from his promises to God.

Solomon's actions were foolish. Since the people of

 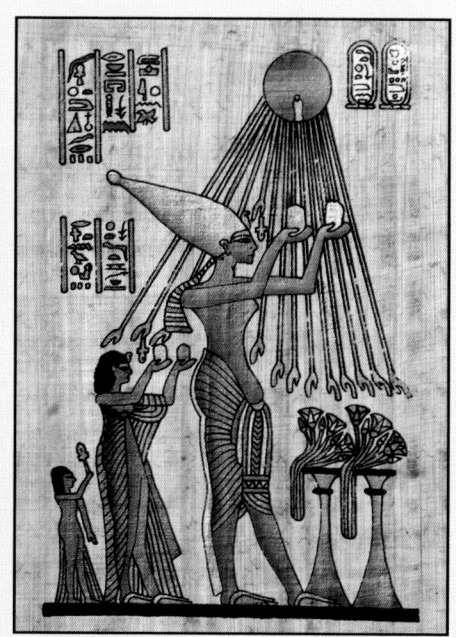

Solomon sinned by permitting the worship of foreign gods, and in participating in such worship at the urging of his numerous wives. (Left) a late Bronze Age representation of Ash'toreth, a Canaanite fertility goddess. (Right) Egyptian papyrus depicting worship of the sun god.

Israel looked up to Solomon as their leader, they too took wives from other lands and other religions. This is not to say that diversity is wrong. In this case, however, it was troublesome.

Since Solomon had many wives from different regions of the East, his house was divided by many different religions. The inhabitants of many countries and cities around Israel believed that a patron god or goddess looked over the country or city in which they lived. If the people did everything required of them by this god, he or she would be appeased and would offer protection to the individual performing the sacrifices and the city or country in which that person lived. When Solomon married wives from these places, they brought their faiths with them. Allowing the worship of their gods is listed as Solomon's greatest offense:

> For Solomon went after Ash'toreth the goddess of the Sido'nians, and after Milcom the abomination of the Am'monites. So Solomon did what was evil in the sight of the Lord, and did not wholly follow the Lord as David his father had done. Then Solomon built a high place for Che'mosh the abomination of Moab, and for Mo'lech the abomination of the Am'monites, on the mountain east of Jerusalem. And so he did for all his foreign wives, who burned incense and sacrificed to their gods. (1 Kings 11:5–8)

The four gods listed here were worshipped in places additional to those listed and have alternate spellings. For instance, the god, Milcom is the same as the god Molech (sometimes spelled Moloch). The second spelling of the name is similar to the Hebrew word for king, melek. It could be that the spelling of the god's name was altered when the passage was transcribed and that he ruled over other gods. Ashtoreth is listed in the Lesser Key of Solomon, another kabbalistic text, as Ashtoreth and is a demon. Chemosh was the national god of Moab and protected that country.

The mountain mentioned is known today as the Mount of Olives. To the Jewish people, it is a sacred place. David fled there when his son, Absalom, tried to take over his kingdom. Later in the Hebrew Bible, Zechariah prophesied from there that the coming Lord of All would begin his reign there. Christians also recognize it from the New Testament.

The passage does not say that Solomon personally worshipped these deities. However, taken in conjunction with the end of the Testament of Solomon, it is clear that at least on one occasion, he offered sacrifices to them. In that text, Solomon married a woman from Moab. Under the instructions of her priests, who worshipped Moloch, she refused to lie in Solomon's bed until he worshipped her gods. Though he remained firm in his convictions, she was persistent and prepared a sacrifice for him to her god, Moloch. Solomon was overcome with lust for the girl and so did as she instructed. After that, he felt he had to build temples to her god and those of his other wives.

The Qur'an offers a different view. In it, Solomon is not faulted for Israel's division:

> "Those [who wished] learned from them what would sow discord between man and wife, but could not harm anybody with it, except with Allah's Permission. They learn what harms them and does not profit them. They knew that he who bought it will have no share in the Hereafter. (Qur'an 1:2)

Here, the people of Israel allow themselves to be led away by choosing to be disobedient to Allah's commands. The two deceptive angels to which the passage refers teach useless and damning magic to the people, but they must announce their deceitfulness to each person wishing to learn, saying: "We are a temptation. So do not disbelieve" (Qur'an 1:2). Thus, the people choose to go astray on their own, rather than being led away by an errant king.

Regardless of whether or not Solomon actually worshipped the gods for whom he created temples, his actions were extremely foolish. From a religious standpoint, Solomon's worship of his wives' gods took his heart and the hearts of his people away from the one true God. From a secular standpoint, the worship of these deities,

Solomon sacrifices to the idols, a painting by the Italian Baroque-era painter Jacopo Amigoni, circa 1700.

offering sacrifices to them, and the construction of places in which they could be worshipped was confusing to the people of Israel.

If the king condoned these practices, then the people would be torn between these new religions and their history. For the Israelites, their worship of the one God was more than a religion. It was their national identity, in which all of their traditions were founded. To undermine that destroyed the unity that bound them together as a people.

These confusing times were compounded by Solomon's own loss of identity. As a shepherd's son, David came from poor and humble beginnings. However, as king, he amassed riches that he used for the good of his people. Solomon built on these, but became so consumed with the building up of Israel and increasing of his own fortune that he forgot the reason behind it—the people. In order to accomplish his goal to establish Israel as a great nation among the others around it, Solomon levied heavy taxes upon the people. He also forced many of them into servitude to complete his many construction projects.

THE PRICE OF EXCELLENCE: TAXATION AND SERVITUDE

Though Solomon's people no doubt still enjoyed the peace that Solomon fostered in Israel and excellent reputation among the other nations he gained for them, they became increasingly aware of the absolutism of his rule. F. W. Farrar summarizes the end of Solomon's reign: "Two deadly evils lurked behind the superficial brilliancy, and wrought incredible harm to king and people—the curse of polygamy and the curse of despotism. The primitive simplicity of the monarchy was nobler, though less showy, than this iridescence of moral stagnancy and luxurious decline." While he once used his power, prestige, and wealth only for the good of his people, Solomon's obsession with building up his kingdom, his wealth, and his harem blinded him to the plight of his people and their sufferings. At the end of Solomon's reign, Israel began to feel the oppression Solomon's excesses placed upon them. Whereas he once lifted the people up for the glory of Israel, he now stood on their backs, elevating himself to bask in his own magnificence.

Solomon's wealth near the end of his reign was clearly recorded: "Now the weight of gold that came to Solomon in one year was six hundred and sixty-six talents of gold, besides that which came from the traders and from the traffic of the merchants and from all the kings of Arabia and from the governors of the land" (1 Kings 10:14–15). Even one talent of gold was a large sum of money. Whereas today, money is measured in denominations like dollars, pounds, yen, and the like, in ancient Israel, large amounts of gold or silver were measured by their weight.

Solomon's 666 talents of gold would weigh a little over 44,048 pounds. The current average cost of one ounce of gold is about $700 per ounce, or about $11,200 per pound in U.S. dollars. Today Solomon's yearly intake of gold would be worth more than $493 million. No differentiation is made between the amount of money Solomon made and the amount of money the kingdom made.

Since he was the king, Solomon would not need to pay taxes. In addition to this large salary, Solomon received gifts from the monarchs of other countries who came seeking his advice. Merchants who sold, traded, or bought goods paid a tax to the crown on each of their transactions as well. All the supplies for his household, including hay for his horses and additional horses, were provided by the officers he had appointed over the regions of Israel. For the privilege of serving Israel and King Solomon, the officers also paid taxes to the king. In order to afford this, the officers passed their burdens on to the people they governed and taxed them heavily.

Solomon covered the streets of Jerusalem in silver and expensive cedar from Lebanon: "And the king made silver as stone and he made cedar as plentiful as the sycamore of the Shephe'lah" (1 Kings 10:27). He made shields out of gold, not to use them, but to store them in the Temple. All of his drinking cups and those used for entertaining his guests in the Hall of the Forest of Lebanon were made of solid gold.

Certainly, all of this would have been impressive to the king's visitors. The Israelites, too, were impressed with the king's glory and that of Israel for much of King Solomon's reign. As F.W. Farrar point points out in his book *Solomon: His Life and Times*, their discontent did not appear all of a sudden, but over time. He writes, "It was only by slow degrees that the glamour of success dissipated, and the nation began to realize the burden of oppression." The price the people paid for the country's prosperity was too high.

As if the taxes placed upon the people were not burden enough, Solomon enslaved them in the service of the kingdom. He did not call this forced labor slavery, because the people would have recognized it as a violation of the laws handed down to Moses in Leviticus. There, God said, "For they are my servants, whom I brought forth out of the land

Cedar trees from Lebanon were used in the construction of the temple in Jerusalem, as well as in Solomon's palace.

of Egypt; they shall not be sold as slaves" (Leviticus 25:42). Under Mosaic Law, slavery was allowed, but the Israelites were not to force one another into servitude: "You may bequeath them to your sons after you, to inherit as a possession for ever; you may make slaves of them, but over your brethren the sons of Israel you shall not rule, one over another, with harshness" (Leviticus 25:46). In the beginning of his reign, Solomon adhered to this prohibition against enslaving his own people.

Instead, he gathered all the people from those countries Israel had destroyed and forced them into labor. "But of the sons of Israel Solomon made no slaves; they were the soldiers, they were his officials, his commanders, his captains, his chariot commanders and his horsemen" (1 Kings 9:22). The difference between slaves and free persons in these two passages is small.

In ancient Israel, once a person was sold into slavery, all the members of that person's family were slaves forever. Slaves could not buy their freedom in their own generation, nor could their descendants. Like a house or a piece of jewelry, slaves were property to be handed down to future generations or sold for a profit. Soldiers, on the other hand, were commissioned to serve only under the ruling monarch. Their families were free, and no one could sell them or bequeath them. Neither group was free, however, since they both had to do as they were instructed by the people who ruled over them.

Excesses of every kind led to Solomon's downfall. They caused his early death despite God's promise of longevity and an end to peace in Israel. Eventually, after Solomon's death and the accession of his son, Solomon's past faults brought the destruction of the united monarchy he and David had worked so hard to build. Israel divided itself into two separate kingdoms, Israel and Judah.

After Solomon's death, his son, Rehoboam became the king of Israel. The people of Israel were tired of the heavy work and tax burdens Solomon had placed upon them and sought relief from the new king. Because he was a new leader, Rehoboam was not prepared to answer them. Therefore, he asked the people to return in three days and sought advice from two groups of men in the meantime.

One of the groups was old and the other young. Since he had grown up with the younger men in his father's palace and knew them better, he took their words to heart and used them when the people came to him a second time: "My father made your yoke heavy, but I will add to your yoke; my father chastised you with whips, but I will chastise you with scorpions" (1 Kings 12:14). When the people heard this, they were enraged. The northern tribes divorced themselves from Judah because Judah remained faithful to the house of David. When Rehoboam tried to send his taskmaster to force the people's return, the taskmaster was stoned to death, and Rehoboam was forced to flee for his life to Judah. The punishment for Solomon's excessive lifestyle was complete.

THE HUMANITY
OF A KING

After learning about Solomon's downfall and the division of Israel that resulted from Solomon's faults, it is easy to wonder why he should be studied at all. In answering this doubt, it is important to remember that all human beings, regardless of their good qualities, are flawed. Instead of allowing Solomon's failings to become an obstacle to learning about him, they should serve as instruments of hope.

Part of Solomon's appeal to modern audiences is that, according to Israel Finkelstein and Neil Asher Silberman, his is "a story of royal manners and aristocratic development, [and] the biblical narrative of Solomon has for centuries provided artists, poets, and theologians with timeless images of royal leadership." Just as people are drawn to fairy tales of kings, queens, princesses, and magical creatures, they are drawn to stories of Solomon and his mighty deeds. Many of the stories written

Because of his human faults, Solomon was unable to fulfill his potential. For Christians, Jesus Christ is the perfection of Solomon and the fulfillment of God's promise. This Byzantine mosaic depicts Jesus descending into Purgatory to free the souls of Adam, Eve, David, and Solomon.

about him sound like fairy tales themselves because they are filled with talking animals and insects, a mechanical throne that seems to come to life on its own whenever the king approaches it, or other seemingly magical or mystical things.

Solomon's wealth, too, is an attraction for many people. He possessed mountains of gold, silver, jewels, horses, and anything else he desired. However, as Solomon learned, money will not buy the things that are really important in life. It cannot buy peace or health or eternal life. Even its value changes through time. Wealth is essentially a fleeting pleasure. However, for many people it is still sought after above all other things because there never seems to be enough money to buy the things they think they need or want in life. Ophir, Solomon's legendary treasure mine, offers a solution to this. With its limitless supply of treasure, surely it would be able to provide "enough," however much that might be. Throughout history, many have lost their lives in the pursuit of Solomon's wealth. Though Ophir has not been found, the search for it is ever hopeful. Treasure hunters seek it to this day, as no doubt they will for many generations to come if it is not found.

Throughout his life, Solomon gave hope to many people and enlightened the masses. Israel Finkelstein and Neil Asher Silberman summarize the longevity of Solomon's reign and the effect he had on the people during his own time when they write: "Forever after, Solomon's rule would be nostalgically recalled as a golden age of spiritual and material fulfillment that might, one day, be experienced again." The skills he used to build the united monarchy of Israel and the spirit with which he accomplished this task are just as important today as they were in Solomon's time. Not everyone possesses great wisdom or limitless wealth, but all people can use the talents and resources they have to build a better world if they overcome their shortcomings.

SOLOMON'S ACCOMPLISHMENTS

In his youth, Solomon was humble. Calling himself a little child, who did not and could not understand the ways of the world, he asked only for wisdom. This unselfish request pleased God because this gift would bring him no personal benefit, but would be of great benefit to Solomon's people. These were God's people, whom he had led out of slavery in Egypt to their own land. However, their past was troubled, and they still suffered from wars and a sense of restlessness. As his name suggested he would, Solomon brought calm and unsurpassed peace to the land of Egypt.

Solomon fulfilled the Israelites' promise to build a permanent dwelling for God among them. He placed the Temple in the center of Jerusalem so that all of the Israelites would have access to it. Though Mosaic Law prevented most people from entering the Temple, those within the city walls would have seen it daily. It would have been a reminder to them of God's presence with them and his plan for their individual lives.

The Temple was a place of pilgrimage for the Jewish people. All the people of Israel, regardless of their proximity to Jerusalem, would have brought or sent their sacrifices and offerings to the Temple in atonement for their sins as prescribed under Mosaic Law. In this way, the Temple served not only as a reminder of the people's faith, but as the very heart of Israel itself.

The Divided Kingdom

Jerusalem remained the capital of Judah when Israel divided. During the period of division, the northern kingdom, which took the name Israel, had three capitals. These were Shechem, Tirzah, and Samaria. At different times, both kingdoms participated in the worship of idols. The northern kingdom fell to the Assyrians in approximately 722 B.C.E. Judah survived a little longer, until the year 586 B.C.E. when Nebuchadnezzar, the king of Babylon, stormed Jerusalem with his armies. He burned the entire city and destroyed Solomon's Temple.

The people of Israel lived in exile until 538 B.C.E. In that year 50,000 Israelites returned to Jerusalem to rebuild the Temple. Several smaller groups returned to Israel in the years following, but the remainder of the restoration took 100 years.

King Solomon reading the Torah, from a late 13th century Hebrew Bible and prayer book. Israel Finkelstein and Neil Asher Silberman note, "[T]he biblical tale of David and Solomon has been read for many centuries as a lesson about how courage, faith, and wisdom can redeem a people from oppression and establish their independence and prosperity."

Before Solomon's reign, and definitely before David's, Israel was not seen favorably among other nations. It was not known for any special achievements or accomplishments. That all changed with the dawn of the Solomonic age. Suddenly, Israel became a place of great culture, an economic giant in the region, and a forerunner in diplomatic relationships. Whereas Israel's past had been filled with wars and conflicts of every kind, its present was peaceful and its ruler exceedingly wise.

Rulers from other countries flocked to Israel in search of answers to their problems. The ancient Roman historian Flavius Josephus describes this in his *Antiquities of the Jews*: "Accordingly there went a great fame all around the neighbouring countries, which proclaimed the virtue and wisdom of Solomon, insomuch that all the kings every-where were desirous to see him, as not giving credit to what was reported, on account of its being almost incredible: they also demonstrated the regard they had for him by the presents they made to him." This passage recounts the general attitude of other countries toward Israel under Solomon's reign.

Countries outside of Israel held little regard for it before Solomon came to power. Therefore, the stories rulers of those countries heard of Solomon and his king-dom were difficult to believe. The Queen of Sheba's visit to King Solomon provides a good example of this attitude toward Israel and how Solomon began to change it.

Solomon presided over his visitors as he did his courts, with confidence and a spirit of understanding. His wisdom surpassed the political arena and encompassed the natural and supernatural worlds as well. He had compassion for his fellow man and rendered just judgments in his court-room. Because of this, Israel gained respect from the countries surrounding it and became a prestigious center of civilization.

Though Solomon reigned during a time of peace, he refortified Jerusalem's walls. These walls served to

A section of fortified wall in present-day Jerusalem. According to 1 Kings 3:1, Solomon strengthened the wall around the ancient city that David had made the capital of his kingdom.

protect the people and buildings within the city, including the Temple. Solomon's palace and the Temple effectively doubled the size of the city. During Solomon's reign, the population also grew rapidly. Because of this immense growth, the city's walls needed to be enlarged and strengthened. By doing this, Solomon increased the peace and security enjoyed by the people.

PITFALLS IN SOLOMON'S REIGN

Solomon completed many useful building projects during his lifetime. Some were used for civic purposes, while others were private buildings constructed for Solomon's use or that of his family. The good he accomplished for Israel was great. However, his failings and the destruction they brought were just as great.

Over time, Solomon became less concerned with the good of his people and more absorbed in selfish pursuits. The editors of *Nelson's Complete Book of Bible Maps and Charts* describe Solomon's reign:

> Solomon's great accomplishments, including the unsurpassed splendor of the Temple which he constructed in Jerusalem, brought him world-wide fame and respect. However, Solomon's zeal for God diminished in his later years, as pagan wives turned his heart away from wholehearted worship of God. As a result, the king with the divided heart leaves behind a divided kingdom, and 1 Kings then traces the twin histories of two sets of kings and two nations of disobedient people.

Great wealth and power often lead to destruction. Solomon's story is a reminder of this fact as much as it is a description of a glorious golden age in Israel's history. His selfishness toward the end of his reign destroyed Israel.

Solomon's downfall was not that he loved his many wives, but that his love for them made him forget what was truly important in his life. Though he was warned by the rules set forth in Leviticus, and then twice again in his visions of God, Solomon refused to listen to prohibitions against having too many wives, collecting too much gold and silver, and horse trading with the Egyptians. Though Solomon obviously regarded these as arbitrary, the restrictions were put into place for the protection of Israel.

Early in their history, the Israelites were slaves to the Egyptians. Trading with them was profitable for Solomon. However, it brought pain to his people. Similarly, the pursuit of gold and silver above all other things made Solomon forget the pain of his people. In fact, through heavy taxation and forced labor, Solomon not only forgot Israel's past sufferings, but also increased its present sufferings.

Solomon is often remembered because of the size of his harem. From the time he began his reign until he died 40 years later, he collected over 1,000 women as part of his royal household. The support of these women and the children they bore was burdensome to Israel because it was so costly. However, their nationalities became an even more important element than their cost in the grand scheme of Solomon's reign. Because they came from different areas, the women brought varied traditions with them. While this increased the perception of Israel as a cultured nation, it also weakened the traditional culture of Israel. This in turn, weakened the country's faith to such an extent that Solomon built places of worship in some of Israel's most sacred locations so that his wives could offer sacrifices to the many gods they brought with them.

Evidence suggests that he, too, may have participated in the worship of these foreign gods. It is not clear whether or not Israel followed Solomon into idolatry while he was king. However, the people's readiness to worship idols in both parts of the divided kingdom after Solomon's death suggests they may have.

What is clear from the accounts presented of Solomon's reign is that the people of Israel looked to him as a leader chosen for them by God. It is also clear that by the end of his reign, he disappointed them. They grew weary of the heavy burden he had placed upon them, and when they could find no relief from it after his death, most of Israel abandoned the house of David from whence Solomon came.

Only two of the original tribes of Israel remained faithful to the royal lineage of David. However, these two tribes were enough to ensure that David's lineage continued so that God's promise that David's house would live forever could be fulfilled. Solomon and his successor were both punished for Solomon's sins against God and the people of Israel. However, as the words of Isaiah reiterate, God's promise would be kept:

> But a shoot shall sprout from the stump of Jesse, and from his roots a bud shall blossom. The spirit of the Lord shall rest upon him: a spirit of wisdom and of understanding, a spirit of counsel and of strength, a spirit of knowledge and of fear of the Lord, and his delight shall be the fear of the Lord. Not by appearance shall he judge, nor by hearsay shall he decide, but he shall judge the poor with justice, and decide aright for the land's afflicted. He shall strike the ruthless with the rod of his mouth, and with the breath of his lips he shall slay the wicked. Justice shall be the band around his waist, and faithfulness a belt upon his hips. (Isaiah 11:1–5)

Wisdom for the Ages

Solomon did not keep his wisdom for himself. Like his building projects, Solomon's writings were done throughout his life. In order to ensure that future generations would be able to reap the benefits of the universal truths of which he had knowledge, Solomon recorded them in written form. The author of 1 Kings writes: "He also uttered three thousand proverbs, and his songs were a thousand and five" (1 Kings 3:32). The King's scribes would have recorded these if he did not write them himself. From this passage, it is evident that in addition to being a wise leader, extraordinary diplomat, husband to many, and exceptional civic leader, Solomon was a prolific writer. Unfortunately, most of Solomon's writings have been lost to the passage of time.

Historically, Solomon has been credited with writing some of Psalms, Proverbs, Ecclesiastes, the Wisdom of Solomon, and the Song of Solomon (also called Canticle of Canticles or Song of Songs). However, today many scholars believe that most of the works supposedly written by Solomon were actually written later and attributed to him because of his fame. The same is true of the lost book Acts of Solomon, which is mentioned in 1 Kings 11:41.

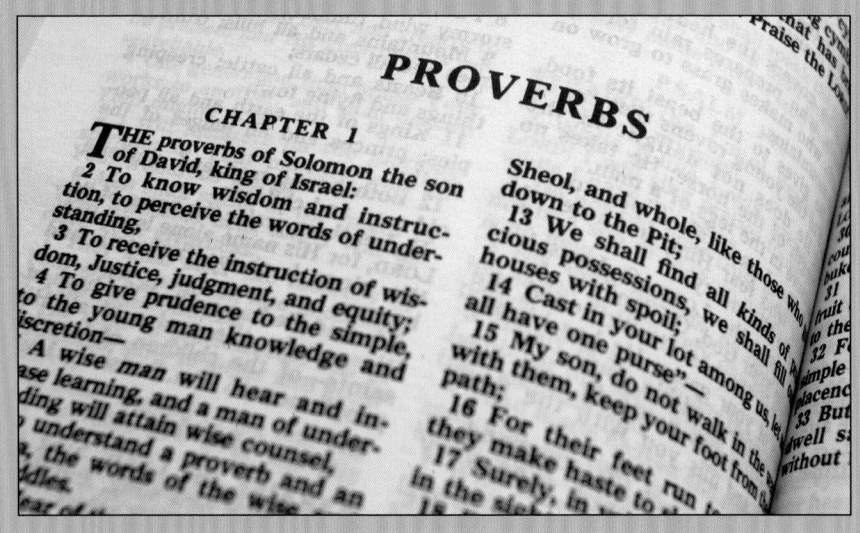

Without knowing Solomon's lineage, the first line of this passage is difficult to understand. It is important to remember that David was the son of Jesse, a shepherd in Bethlehem, and Solomon was the son of David. A stump is what is left of a tree when it is cut down. Normally, it does not yield new branches, but in this case, it will. The branch of Solomon was cut from the tree because of his sins, but according to the prophet, David's lineage will not end with him. The future ruler promised in Isaiah is the fulfillment of all Solomon could have been. His wisdom will be as great as Solomon's if not greater, but he will not be overcome by his humanity.

In order to learn the lessons Solomon's story provides, a student must examine his full humanity, both good and bad. His generosity toward the people of Israel in the beginning of his reign teaches the importance of acting kindly toward others and using one's gifts and talents in the service of others. His downfall warns of the pitfalls of prideful selfishness. Both parts taken together provide examples of how the actions and decisions of one person can affect many. While these are all valuable lessons, perhaps Solomon's greatest teaching is the importance of truly knowing oneself and acting according to the nature of one's best self. If he had known his faults, Solomon would not have led Israel astray. Instead, he would have fulfilled his promises and continued in his destiny to bring peace and unity to Israel.

Notes

page 13: "See! The blood..." Hayyim Nahman Bialik, *And It Came to Pass: Legends and Stories About King David and King Solomon* (New York: Hebrew Publishing, 1938), p. 74.

page 13: "Under Solomon's rule..." Louis Ginzberg, *Legends of the Jews*, trans. Henrietta Szold and Paul Radin, vol. 2 (Philadelphia: The Jewish Publication Society, 2003), p. 978.

page 13: "But Solomon's wealth..." Ginzberg, *Legends of the Jews*, p. 958.

page 15: "Whoever saw boiled eggs..." Bialik, *And It Came to Pass: Legends and Stories About King David and King Solomon*, p. 67.

page 21: "The story of David..." Israel Finkelstein and Neil Asher Silberman, *David and Solomon: In Search of the Bible's Sacred Kings and the Roots of the Western Tradition* (New York: Free Press, 2006), p. 3.

page 25: "but all of his attempts..." Finkelstein and Silberman, *David and Solomon: In Search of the Bible's Sacred Kings and the Roots of the Western Tradition*, p. 108.

page 33: "The biblical story..." Finkelstein and Silberman, *David and Solomon: In Search of the Bible's Sacred Kings and the Roots of the Western Tradition*, p. 142.

page 34: "The biblical description of..." Finkelstein and Silberman, *David and Solomon: In Search of the Bible's Sacred Kings and the Roots of the Western Tradition*, p. 151.

page 39: "The eagle alone..." Bialik, *And It Came to Pass: Legends and Stories About King David and King Solomon*, p. 78.

page 39: "I, Solomon, son of David..." Bialik, *And It Came to Pass: Legends and Stories About King David and King Solomon*, p. 79.

page 45: "but all these..." Roland de Vaux, *Ancient Israel: Its Life and Institutions*, trans. John McHugh (New York: McGraw-Hill, 1961), p. 116.

page 45: "From some passages..." de Vaux, *Ancient Israel: Its Life and Institutions*, p. 115.

page 55: "As Islam spread through..." Finkelstein and Silberman, *David and Solomon: In Search of the Bible's Sacred Kings and the Roots of the Western Tradition*, p. 254.

page 55: "The stories of Solomon in..." Finkelstein and Silberman, *David and Solomon: In Search of the Bible's Sacred Kings and the Roots of the Western Tradition*, p. 175.

page 58: "Then the queen began..." Ginzberg, *Legends of the Jews*, p. 958.

page 60: "forasmuch as the spirit..." Stephen Ashe, ed., *The Qabalah: The Testament of Solomon* (Glastonbury: Glastonbury, 2007), p. 75.

page 61: "Solomon's image promises security..." Finkelstein and Silberman, *David and Solomon: In Search of the Bible's Sacred Kings and the Roots of the Western Tradition*, p. 176–77.

page 63: "but his harem and his palaces..." F. W. Farrar, *Solomon: His Life and Times* (Whitefish, MT: Kessinger, 2004), p. 63.

page 67: "The cubit traditionally..." Kingsley, *God's Gold: A Quest for the Lost Temple Treasures of Jerusalem* (New York: Harper Collins, 2007), p. 271.

page 70: "Take, O Solomon, king..." Ashe, *The Qabalah: The Testament of Solomon*, p. 17.

page 72: "Among the great achievements..." Ginzberg, *Legends of the Jews*, p. 978.

page 73: "Kings that have once..." Farrar, *Solomon: His Life and Times*, p. 105.

page 73: "On each of the six..." Bialik, *And It Came to Pass: Legends and Stories About King David and King Solomon*, p. 113.

page 74: "On the lowest step..." Bialik, *And It Came to Pass: Legends and Stories About King David and King Solomon*, p. 113.

page 76: "The Jebusite water-shaft..." Bruce M. Metzger and Michael D. Coogan, eds., *The Oxford Guide to People and Places of the Bible* (New York: Oxford University Press, 2001), p. 128.

page 76: "that each successive city..." Victor H. Matthews, *A Brief History of Ancient Israel* (Louisville, KY: Westminster John Knox, 2002), p. 47.

page 77: "they contribute to the royal..." Carol Meyers, "Kinship and Kingship," in *The Oxford History of the Biblical World* (New York: Oxford University Press, 1998), p. 248.

page 83: "It is a vivid lesson..." Finkelstein and Silberman, *David and Solomon: In Search of the Bible's Sacred Kings and the Roots of the Western Tradition*, p. 9.

page 88: "Two deadly evils lurked..." Farrar, *Solomon: His Life and Times*, p. 140.

page 90: "It was only by slow..." Farrar, *Solomon: His Life and Times*, p. 70.

page 93: "a story of royal manners..." Finkelstein and Silberman, *David and Solomon: In Search of the Bible's Sacred Kings and the Roots of the Western Tradition*, p. 153.

page 95: "Forever after, Solomon's rule..." Finkelstein and Silberman, *David and Solomon: In Search of the Bible's Sacred Kings and the Roots of the Western Tradition*, p. 8.

page 97: "[T]he biblical tale..." Finkelstein and Silberman, *David and Solomon: In Search of the Bible's Sacred Kings and the Roots of the Western Tradition*, p. 3.

page 97: "Accordingly there went..." Flavius Josephus, *Antiquities of the Jews in The Works of Josephus*, trans. William Whiston (Lynn, MA: Hendrickson, 1982), p. 181.

page 99: "Solomon's great accomplishments..." Thomas Nelson, *Nelson's Complete Book of Bible Maps and Charts*. (Nashville: Thomas Nelson, 1982), p. 111.

Depiction of King Solomon in stained glass at the Cathedral of Chartres in France.

Glossary

absolutism—a political system in which the ruler has unlimited power.

acumen—skillful insight.

atonement—payment for wrongdoing.

chastise—to punish, especially bodily as by beating.

concubine—a substitute wife or a woman who lives with a man to whom she is not married.

deductive reasoning—finding the cause of something by its effects.

despotism—a government in which the ruler has absolute power.

Deuteronomist—the author of the historical books of the Bible between Joshua and 2 Kings.

excavation—the process of digging and removing material from the earth, especially in an archaeological expedition or journey.

Islam—the religion followed by the Muslim people based on the Qur'an.

Judaism—the religion followed by the Jewish people based on the Torah and the Talmud.

lineage—family tree.

monarchy—a form of government in which the ruler of a country is a king or queen.

nomad—a person without a permanent home.

polygamy—the practice of being married to more than one person at a time.

progeny—offspring; heirs; a person's children.

prolific—producing many works of art or other intellectual products in a short amount of time; especially used when referring to writing.

servitude—a state of being in which a person is not free and is forced into labor.

sluice gates—an opening in a canal that allows a specific amount of water to enter; can be opened or closed to regulate water flow.

Further Reading

BOOKS FOR YOUNG READERS

Bialik, Hayyim Nahman. *And It Came to Pass: Legends and Stories About King David and King Solomon*. 1938. Reprint, Whitefish, MT: Kessinger, 2007.

Metzger, Bruce M., and Michael D. Coogan, eds. *The Oxford Guide to People and Places of the Bible*. New York: Oxford University Press, 2001.

Oberman, Sheldon. *Solomon and the Ant: And Other Jewish Folktales*. Honesdale, PA: Boyds Mills, 2006.

Sherman, Joseph. *Your Travel Guide to Ancient Israel*. Minneapolis, MN: Lerner, 2003.

Thomas Nelson. *Nelson's Complete Book of Bible Maps and Charts: Old and New Testaments*. Nashville: Thomas Nelson, 1982.

Wilson, Neil S., and Linda K. Taylor. *Tyndale Handbook of Bible Charts and Maps*. Carol Stream, IL: Tyndale House, 2001.

BOOKS FOR ADULTS

Cheyne, T. K. *Job and Solomon or the Wisdom of the Old Testament*. 1887. Reprint. Whitefish, MT: Kessinger, 2007.

De Vaux, Roland. *Ancient Israel*. Translated by John McHugh. New York: McGraw-Hill, 1961.

Farrar, F. W. *Solomon: His Life and Times*. Reprint. Whitefish, MT: Kessinger, 2004.

Finkelstein, Israel, and Neil Asher Silberman. *David and Solomon: In Search of the Bible's Sacred Kings and the Roots of the Western Tradition*. New York: Free Press, 2006.

Kingsley, Sean. *God's Gold: A Quest for the Lost Temple Treasures of Jerusalem*. Harper Collins: New York, 2007.

Matthews, Victor H. *A Brief History of Ancient Israel*. Louisville, KY: Westminster John Knox, 2002.

Scott, Steven K. *The Richest Man Who Ever Lived: King Solomon's Secrets to Success, Wealth, and Happiness*. Strawberry Hills, Australia: Currency, 2006.

Whiston, William, trans. *The Works of Josephus: Complete and Unabridged*. Lynn, MA: Hendrickson, 1980.

Internet Resources

http://www.archpark.org.il

> Originating in Israel, this site offers an exploration of historical and archaeological evidence relating to both the first and second Temples.

http://www.biblicalarchaeology.org

> This site provides an excellent resource for examining archaeological evidence relating the Old and New Testaments. It is the online home of the bimonthly magazine *Biblical Archaeology Review*. Journal contents are searchable, and past journal articles can be viewed for a fee.

http://www.BibleInterp.com

> This site, designed to bringing recent biblical scholarship to a general audience, includes news reports as well as hundreds of archived articles by top scholars.

http://www.BibleMap.org

> With this unique, interactive site, users can type in a Bible book and chapter, and all geographical references contained in that passage will be flagged on a map.

http://www.HolyLandPhotos.org

This site, created by Dr. Carl Rasmussen of Bethel University, includes thousands of free, high-resolution photographs of places from all over the biblical world.

http://www.jewishencyclopedia.com

This searchable site provides access to the public domain version of the 12-volume *Jewish Encyclopedia*, originally published 1901–1906. It provides several general articles on Solomon and his accomplishments.

http://www.kingsolomonsgate.com

King Solomon's Gate details archaeology's attempts to find evidence in support of the existence of Solomon and other key figures in the Bible.

http://www.myjewishlearning.com

This Web site provides well-written historical and scholarly information about Judaism.

http://www.newadvent.org/cathen/14135b.htm

New Advent is a searchable encyclopedia. This link goes directly to the article on Solomon. While it is not extremely detailed, the article provides an overview of the subject.

http://www.sacred-texts.com

The Internet Sacred Text Archive has an enormous repository of electronic texts about religion, mythology, legends and folklore, and occult and esoteric topics. Texts related to Solomon include the works of Josephus and *The Legends of the Jews*, by Louis Ginzberg.

http://www.Templeinstitute.org

This site explores the historical significance of the first
and second Temples in Jerusalem. It also looks forward to
a time when a third Temple can be built and examines the
importance of such a Temple to the Jewish people.

http://www.Templemount.org

Though not exclusively dedicated to Solomon's Temple,
this site contains several good articles on the Temple from
varying religious points of view.

http://www.torahscience.org

This searchable site offers articles concerning Solomon's
wisdom and the science of kabbalistic sources.

Index

Numbers in **bold italics** refer to captions.

Illustration Credits

JENNIFER VANCE currently lives in Birmingham, Alabama. She received both her BA and MA in English from Northwestern State University of Louisiana. Her publications include three articles in *The Dictionary of Literary Biography*, volume 292. This is her first book.